NEW PERSPECTIVES ON THE **GOLD RUSH**

The Turnagain Nugget. In 1937 Alice Shea found this nugget wedged in a boulder while walking along Turnagain Creek to her husband's claim in northern British Columbia. It is the largest existing gold nugget found in the province, weighing 1642 grams or 52 troy ounces. BC's Department of Mines bought the nugget for $1500 and displayed it at the 1939 World's Fair in San Francisco. Today, this rock is worth more than $75,000.
RBCM 990.65.1

NEW PERSPECTIVES ON THE
GOLD RUSH

Edited by Kathryn Bridge

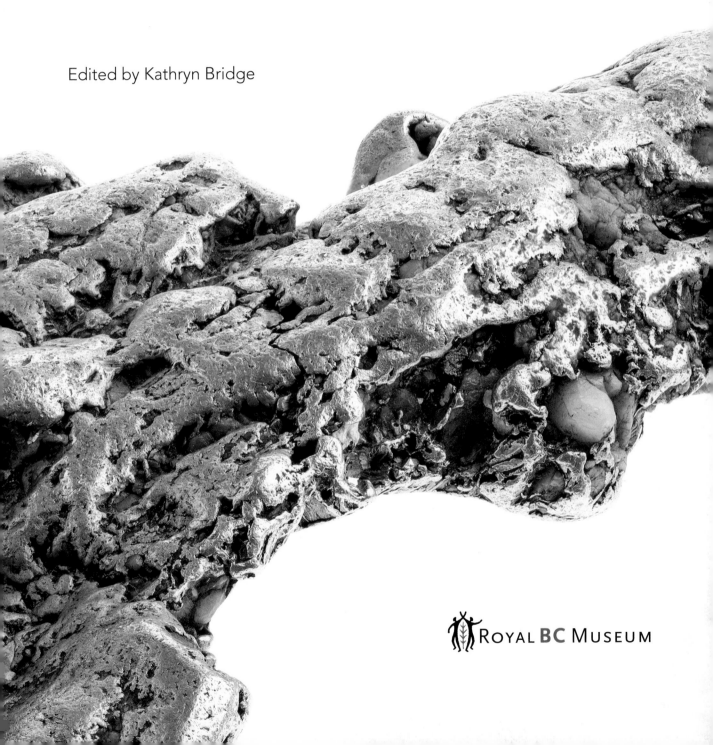

ROYAL **BC** MUSEUM

The Cariboo Wagon Road running through the Fraser River Canyon in the 1860s. Unknown photographer; BCA D-08066

Wheel and flumes at the Davis claim,
Williams Creek, on June 15, 1867.
Frederick Dally photograph;
BCA A-00558

CONTENTS

Henry Nathan Jr operated a general store and commission agency in Victoria for gold seekers heading to the Fraser River. At his store miners could stock up on supplies and obtain a mining license. In 1871 Nathan became the first Jewish member of British Columbia's legislative assembly, representing Victoria. RBCM HH1988.6.1

Label from a portable gold scale brought from California. RBCM 990.19.229

Foreword

The Honourable Judith Guichon

THERE ARE FEW PERIODS IN BRITISH COLUMBIA'S HISTORY that have had as much impact in shaping our province as we know it today than that of the gold rush. So much of British Columbia's development can be linked back to those early explorers and adventurers who came as young men looking for gold, new frontiers, excitement and adventure. Their restless spirit propelled these fortune seekers to the province's interior, paving the way for development and infrastructure. Those pioneers who came, explored and then stayed to build communities, laid the foundation for the civil, genteel lifestyle that we are all fortunate to enjoy today. My family's own story is linked to this same attraction.

The ranch I have lived on for more than 40 years was first established in the 1870s by Laurent and Joseph Guichon, who as very young men came from France, lured by stories of gold. They had missed the California rush and so continued north to Barkerville and staked claims not far from Lytton and in Barkerville. Eventually they became packers, ferrying supplies to the miners. The road to the interior led the Guichon brothers to the Nicola River Valley in search of land to overwinter their livestock. As I so often tell schoolchildren who visit my ranch, they came for the gold but they stayed for the grass.

The gold rush brought a previously unseen wave of immigration to the province, drawing men and some women from around the world in search of new fortune. Many of these gold seekers, like the young Guichon brothers, would settle permanently on this new land. Their presence would go on to influence the culture, landscape and overall future of British Columbia. *New Perspectives on the Gold Rush* brings this significant period in our province's formation to life. It gives us an understanding of the lifestyle, the tools, and even the hopes and dreams, of these early adventurers. It was the lure of finding that great golden treasure that was the impetus to build this province. This book gives readers the opportunity to get a true sense of the experiences of these venturesome and optimistic fortune seekers.

The Honourable Judith Guichon, OBC
Lieutenant-Governor of British Columbia

Foreword

Coralee Oakes

BARKERVILLE, the largest historic town in western North America, is one of the most significant sites in British Columbia. The appeal of the place is its rich and living gold-mining heritage – a connection to the pioneers who built our province: the dreamers, visionaries and builders who came together to forge communities. Old-fashioned streets with boardwalks fronting historic wooden stores and businesses hold a particular interest for today's families. Many people fondly remember visiting Barkerville as children and now bring their young ones to experience the magic that this restored town has to offer. Images of Barkerville dominate our "memory" of the gold rush. The town, as many know, was the heart of the Cariboo gold rush, but it also stands as a monument to the many gold rushes in British Columbia.

Now, thanks to the imagination of curators and scholars, and the generosity of numerous museums, including the famous Museo del Oro in Bogota, Colombia, the story of gold rushes has been opened up far beyond the local geography and, in a way, beyond the knowledge of historians. The story is revealed as a more complex narrative. It shows First Peoples and Chinese immigrants as integral participants in shaping our country's history; it shows persecuted people finding safety; women working and living in hard circumstances alongside miners; the legacy of gold-rush architecture; and the ability of place to conjure powerful memories. It is this interconnectedness that the writers in this book ultimately reveal.

I am delighted that the Royal BC Museum has partnered with the Canadian Museum of History and the Museo del Oro on this project. I am grateful to CMH Director General Mark O'Neil and Director Marc Blais for their immense support in the creation of the exhibition that spawned this book. This project owes a great debt to Museo del Oro Director Maria Alicia Uribe Villegas and to her colleagues who agreed to loan some of the their museum's finest treasures. I am also grateful to Consul General Jairo Clopatofsky of Colombia and Canadian Ambassador to Colombia Her Excellency Carmen Sylvain for their full cooperation and support.

To all who have contributed – the many people and organizations across British Columbia, Canada and indeed the world – I am personally very grateful.

Coralee Oakes
Minister of Community, Sport and Cultural Development

Foreword

Jack Lohman

ASK ANY CHILD what happened in British Columbia during the 19th century and they are likely to draw a blank. History has settled and the sense of adventure, so much at the forefront of what drove men and women to come to Canada's west coast, has vanished. If they see anything of Canada's past, it is of the contested legacy of what went on.

To understand that history, we need to reimagine it. And what better adventure than the thrill of the gold rush. It has all the qualities of a tactical video game: riches, chance, skill, danger. There is a terrain that makes enormous demands on the player. There are characters of all sorts – adventurers, con men, wide-eyed hopefuls and the doggedly committed. All arrive at once – you've got to be quick in a gold rush – each one desperate to be the first to succeed beneath bright skies that shimmer with the promise of gold.

BC's gold rushes are forgotten events. The fame of the Klondike, "The Last Great Gold Rush", has tended to occlude a long earlier history, of gold found in California and Australia, and gold in British Columbia. But the Klondike gold rush of 1897 marked the pinnacle of a half-century of greed, ambition, fantasy and dreams. There is a larger coastal history to consider, from the forty-niners who followed the California trail in 1849 to the Fraser River miners of the late 1850s. Gold shaped the entire west coast as the last frontier of North American exploration.

That other history is also a world history. Gold rushes feel intensely local. They transform places such as the Cariboo. But they tell, in fact, global stories of the shifting relations between the world's peoples and places. Who are these adventurers? It is a question that reveals many histories: of First Nations participants, of immigrants from China who stayed on to build the Canadian Pacific Railway, of those seeking better lives for themselves. Gold communities bring together diverse cultures and widely different social expectations. They are an intense history of Canada in miniature. These sudden populations throw up particular conflicts and create unexpected bonds, both among people and with the lands they get to know. What we might guess took place is not always, in this context of realistic gain and unrealistic hope, what plays out among the pan-handles. Gold rushes offer a particular, and particularly revealing, Canadian history.

Many of those caught up in the gold rush were ordinary men and women. Their stories emerge from the archive with poignancy and grit, and it is fitting that the continent's margins welcomed the marginal in society. These modest folk would be surprised to find themselves judged as powerful colonizers. It was their exclusion by the potentates of Europe and the Far East, of North and South America that drove them on, part of a larger movement of settlement from outside but lost to its rewards. Few managed even in the seeming ease of discovering gold to garner any significant wealth. Yet their role was important to our history.

The very appeal of gold has its own history. We cannot just assume its importance. Why gold? Found in Bulgaria, the earliest known gold artifacts are 6000 years old, and in the cultures of ancient Egypt and South America, gold carried powerful ritual significance. Soft, pliable and non-corrosive, gold is easy to work and it endures. It is also all too easily melted down and transported. Gold is, therefore, the site of world conflict: war over ownership, buying power, beautiful objects coveted and inseparable, to our eyes at least, from their monetary value. We can see how myths around it become so powerful: from the Gold Mountain of Chinese folklore to King Midas's touch to El Dorado. Whether we are admiring exquisitely worked anthropomorphic ornaments from Colombia or the mythic potency inscribed in a Bill Reid sculpture, gold announces its importance.

Canada's history might seem far from such myths, but it is not. Visions of gold are among the stories of new-found wealth people brought with them when they confronted the landscape of North America. The mountains and the sea frame British Columbia with a majesty everyone can see. But there were surely hidden glories too, and as we still know today, that beauty comprises other less visible riches: contemplative, environmental, economic. What Canada is, is both overt and hidden.

The country's early Confederation poets were excited by this double essence, capturing its qualities in many of their poems. Wilfred Campbell pays tribute to the wintry stillness of "lonely hidden bays, moon-lit, ice-rimmed ... haunted by shadowy shores". No longer remaking the landscape through the lens of Europe, Campbell sees Canada afresh – a place of undiscovered treasures; a living, burgeoning presence to be explored; an opportunity. Here is a portrait of a country about to be born, to take to the air. There are dangers to be sure, but there is paradise too. Campbell conveys how exciting it was to see Canada's potential. His imagination ran towards the future, dazzled by nature's plenty.

This is the spirit of the gold rush.

Jack Lohman
CEO, Royal British Columbia Museum

This British Columbia Express Company stagecoach was recovered from the bush and restored by the historic O'Keefe Ranch, which was founded during the BC gold rush. BC Express was established by Francis Barnard and two other men in 1871. Ten years before, Barnard had started up a pony express service from Lillooet to the gold fields, which he expanded with wagons and, by 1867, extended south all the way to Victoria. Four years later BC Express Co. assumed this service. Along the four-day trip from Yale to Barkerville, roadhouses every 18 miles supplied meals and fresh horses. Some towns still carry their roadhouse names, measured in miles from Lillooet (mile 0); the largest, 100 Mile House, is 100 miles (160 km) from Lillooet. (Stagecoach courtesy of the O'Keefe Ranch.)

NOON ON THE FRAZER.
OUR BIVOUAC BEYOND THE

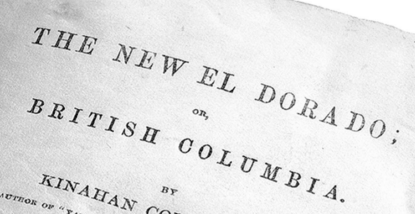

THE NEW EL DORADO;

OR,

BRITISH COLUMBIA.

BY

KINAHAN CORNWALLIS,

AUTHOR OF "YARRA YARRA," "HOWARD PLUNKETT," &c., &c.

To the clime of Columbia, Britain's new born,
Where the rays of the sun gladly usher the morn,
And the landscape deck out with a smile;
Where the hearts of the countless beat hopefully high,
And gold doth the moments beguile;
Where the frown of the mountains, the blue of the sky,
Contrast in their beauty with forest and plain;
Where the green perfumed prairie rolls in the breeze,
And mankind ever struggle for gain;
Where the sight of the ore even fails to appease
Man's inordinate yearning for gold,—
Still making each eagerly struggle the more
For the treasure ungather'd—untold.
'Tis a land of exuberant plenty and joy;
Go, ye children of cities, by fortune opprest,
Where gold may be gathered which knows no alloy;
Far and wide doth it lie on that beautiful shore,
May it gladden and laurel the pathway of time
'Tis the wanderer to traverse who reaps from its mine.
Left the bauble of earth;—'tis the gift of the clime,
Of millions the spoil,—It is mine—It is thine.

A MAP AND ILLUSTRATION BY THE AUTHOR.

LONDON:

CAUTLEY NEWBY, PUBLISHER,

30, WELBECK STREET.

1858.

FAR FROM HOME

by W.H.D. [1]

Where mighty waters foam and boil
And rushing torrents roar,
In Fraser River's northern soil
Lies hid the golden ore.

Chorus (repeated after each verse)
Far from home, far from home
On Fraser River's shore
We labour hard, so does our bard,
To dig the golden ore.

Far, far from home we Miners roam,
We feel its joys no more.
These we have sold for yellow gold
On Fraser River's shore.

In cabins rude, our daily food
Is quickly counted o'er.
Beans, bread, salt meat is all we eat—
And the cold earth is our floor.

Lonely our lives—no mothers', wives',
Or sisters' love runs o'er
When home we come at set of sun
To greet us at the door.

At night we smoke, then crack a joke,
Try cards 'til found a bore.
Our goodnight said, we go to bed
To dream of home once more.

With luck at last, our hardships past,
We'll head for home once more,
And greet the sight with wild delight
Of California's shore.

And once on shore, we never more
Will roam through all our lives:
A home we'll find, just to our mind,
And call our sweethearts wives.

Miners used a blow pan, like this one, to separate gold dust from sand. There are 21 grams of gold dust in this pan.
RBCM 964.3495.6a

Introduction

Kathryn Bridge

COMPOSED IN JULY 1859 by an unknown American miner on Emory's Bar on the Fraser River, these lyrics evoke the loneliness of a homesick gold seeker, surviving on basic food rations, sleeping in a rude shelter, yet living in comradeship with other like-minded miners. They reinforce what we assume to be the daily experiences of a miner – hard work, sacrifice, boredom and harsh living. But the gold rush, as a historical chapter, produced outcomes that the solitary miner "far from home" could never have imagined.

Digging ditches on the river's edge and building flumes to divert water into rocker boxes created social and environmental consequences. The actions of gold seekers altered the natural gravel banks of the rivers and disrupted spawning salmon. Their mining claims, mining gear and miners themselves blocked indigenous people from access to the river. Overlapping and competing mining stakes could erupt in violence, because the multiple cultures of the gold miners set difference as a rationale for racism. Colonial assumptions of the right to govern and to create and uphold the law, to claim and change the land set in motion events that coloured successive generations. Our retrospective understanding of the gold rush is layered by both individual and collective actions in the past that have been woven into narratives and preserved over time.

Not all miners headed "for home once more". Of the many who stayed, some founded businesses, others settled down with First Nations women, or built ranches, or, became active in politics, and some led quiet lives. Whether these gold seekers went home or stayed behind, whether they made their mark or left little trace, their collective actions helped to shape this place into the province of British Columbia.

In 1858 a great wave of humanity poured into the area we now call British Columbia. By all accounts 30,000 gold seekers – mostly men – arrived within the first few months and many others followed over the next five years. News of gold – of a New El Dorado – spurred a rush that changed forever the ways of life for First Nations inhabitants and those already settled in or around fur-trading posts. Most of the early gold seekers arrived at Fort Victoria, Vancouver Island, via ocean-going vessels from San Francisco. From there they journeyed across the Strait of Georgia to the mainland and on to Fort Yale, at the head of navigation on the Fraser River. Thousands more came overland from California, through Oregon and Washington territories, and followed native trails and river courses northward to the gold fields.

The gold rush has received much attention from historians and local history buffs.[2] Books, websites, museums and historical highway signs

Hand-forged tools for mining by hand: a curved fork for clawing rock surfaces, and shovel-like implements for scraping and digging in crevices. RBCM 965.5, RBCM 2014.188.1, RBCM 2014.188.2

tell stories about the rush and the movements of gold seekers north along the Fraser River into the Cariboo. They also talk about the mini-rushes that followed along the Fraser's tributaries, in Atlin, along the Omineca and Similkameen rivers, in the Kootenays and at the Leech River on Vancouver Island. Barkerville, now a national heritage site in the Cariboo, along with a series of small settlements – the original historical stopping houses for changing horses along the Cariboo Wagon Road – and towns such as Lytton, Lillooet, Spences Bridge and Boston Bar are reminders of this transitional chapter in British Columbia's history. Place names associated with the gold rush are fast disappearing with depopulation, but a few are being incorporated into current usage. For instance, Emory Creek (where the unknown miner wrote the song) is now the name of a campground there. Kanaka Bar, named for Hawaiian miners who worked there, became the name of a First Nations reserve. In years past, the Province supported and established historical stops of interest that preserved homes and ranches of the immediate post-rush period as heritage properties. Places like Hat Creek

Ranch (near Cache Creek), Ashcroft Manor and Cottonwood House survive in their architecture and settings as physical reminders of the scale of settler achievements.[3] Tourism BC promotes the Gold Rush Trail, and the New Pathways to Gold Society supports economic growth through heritage tourism, First Nations reconciliation, community projects and events.

For years, stories of who struck it rich and who lost it all dominated popular interpretations of the gold rush: Billy Barker, Cariboo Cameron, Judge Matthew Baillie Begbie, lost gold mines, murder mysteries, hanging trees. The emphasis was on personality rather than the society as a whole. But by studying the actions and interconnectedness of a wider range of historical players, new perspectives emerge. Several areas of study present rich opportunities. The "instant" society created by a gold rush held very distinct characteristics and its own complexities. Most visibly, the population was about 90 per cent men. White women – the wives, daughters, business owners and, yes, miners – lived in a dominantly male society. Likewise, most members of this colonial society were very young, the average age well below 30. Intergenerational relationships would be remote, maintained through letters back home. How might such an age-defined male-dominated society have challenged its members?[4]

Gold seekers shared a dream to strike it rich, but was that dream enough to overcome the differences presented by their cohort, or the raw country? For it was also a multicultural society. English was not the only language spoken – Spanish, Chinese, French or German were likely heard on the trails, on the gravel bars of the river and in Victoria and the other settlements. How might you function in a setting where you did not understand the languages spoken by others around you? Literacy in English – to read the newspapers, to understand the regulations – would have been crucial. And what of different customs? Would you find common ground? Likewise, class differences among gold seekers would have been apparent, but how much did this guide the interactions of miners? Not everyone chose to search for gold. Merchants established businesses catering to miners; doctors and lawyers provided medical and legal services; engineers and architects built roads and structures.

How the gold rush society operated, how people from different classes, cultures and races interacted provides some of the subject matter for this book. The ten essays contained offer new insights about the gold-rush years. Recent internet postings of digitally scanned historical records have opened avenues of research not previously available. Small references buried within published government and private written records are now searchable.

But historical records still favour the literate. Most of the gold seekers left no personal records, their presence known only as names on mining licenses or in statistics collected by gold commissioners and government agents. It is not easy locating the evidence, and then judging how to use it. Understanding the average person of that time remains a challenge for historians, though more balanced and thoughtful analyses of the gold rush in recent decades have enabled new insights and more inclusive histories.[5] But studying differences within the multiracial, multicultural cohort of gold seekers remains less explored, while the perspectives of the resident First Nations are almost entirely unacknowledged.

Hand-made miner's tunnel cart used in Barkerville in the 1860s. RBCM 971.244.1A-H

The gold seekers trespassed upon traditional lands of the First Nations, whose populations on the coast and along the Fraser River (Coast Salish, Nlaka'pamux, Stl'atl'imc, Tsilhqot'in and Secwepemc) greatly exceeded that of the gold seekers.[6] They were there, contributory and visible, yet seldom mentioned in personal records of the day and mostly ignored in governmental decision-making. Oral histories written down by or for anthropologists in the 1890s or later, focused on recording traditional cultures and ignored the contemporary circumstances faced by the First Nations.[7] These records do not describe details of everyday existence in a world suddenly filled with outsiders focused on gold and living though the massive changes that would come within a single generation, nor was there any acknowledgement of land ownership. The publication of First Nations perspectives augmented by third-party written and visual sources is long overdue.

In more recent times, academic research has asked (but not always answered) many of the broad questions: What was the effect of the gold rush on the development of the province and how does it fit into 19th-century world migrations? Did the gold rush enable colonial rule or challenge it? Did this society of men enable less rigid enactment of gender roles? Did the few women in the gold rush experience freedoms, and if so, did this open doors to new opportunities – or was it the opposite? How did individuals in this multicultural society deal with barriers of language, customs, social expectations and understandings? What long-term impacts upon the land can now be measured as a result of the gold rush? Might infrastructure development have occurred differently if British Columbia had never experienced a gold rush? Did the gold rush disrupt a more orderly intention to establish land treaties with First Nations? What was the impact of mixed marriages and alliances in the post-gold-rush society? How do we learn about the lives of people of whom so little is documented in archives but by their numbers must have left an imprint? What was it like to be a Chinese miner facing racism? Did the gold rush in BC prove to be a lesson for other jurisdictions in maintaining law and order, or leave a legacy in legislation, liberal thinking and wider world consciousness? How do we situate BC's gold rush in relation to colonialism, nationalism and trans-border economies?

Moose-hide jacket belonging to overlander Richard Henry Alexander. In 1862, Alexander walked across Canada for seven months to reach the Cariboo and then rafted down the Fraser River to the coast.
RBCM 967.149.1

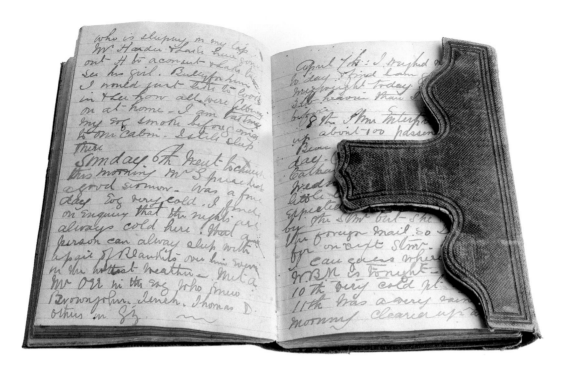

Diary of James Nelles, from Grimsby Ontario, who walked overland to the Cariboo in 1862. BCA MS-0843

The gold rush occurred just before the downward swing of British imperialism. The colonies of Vancouver Island (created in 1849) and British Columbia (in 1858) would together in 1871 become the sixth province of the Dominion of Canada. But the mind-set of imperial rule, and the actions of colonial governance prevailed, vestiges we still recognize today, setting the stage for modernity.

Gold seekers came from almost all points on the globe. For many, the gold rush was just that – a short, intense period in which to find wealth and return home. Many went home penniless; some died trying to strike it rich. For the First Nations people living in the area, the gold rush was an intimate experience. Some participated as miners, all endured racism, and many suffered violent acts committed by gold seekers and often retaliated. Understanding the multiple perspectives of the many rather than the few remains a challenge for historians and others who seek to learn about our past.

The following essays incorporate new ways of looking at historical evidence. By examining how something is said in a diary or government correspondence and noting what is not said, by comparing sources for commonalities and differences, and by taking advantage of online search capabilities, it is now possible to see patterns that enable us to interrogate the sources themselves, and in so doing gain new insights about this pivotal time in our history.

Rereading known sources with new intentions is how we build upon or break down our assumptions and improve our understanding of the past. Historical research is not confined to written or visual sources but also incorporates intangible heritage – language, social customs and oral traditions. Clues to the past are also held in material culture, the objects and buildings people make and use in daily life. All of these sources inform the essays in this book.

The authors of these essays are museum curators, historians, heritage professionals and educators. We asked them to pick a topic that interests

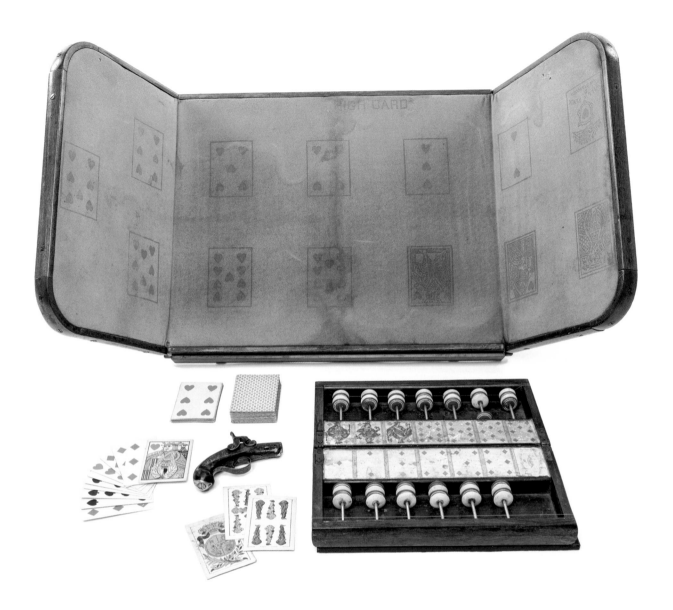

Gambling presented another opportunity to make a fortune ... or lose it. Before 1870, faro was the most popular gambling game, not poker. Players place their bets on the 13 cards painted on the board. The dealer draws two cards – the first card pays the house; the second the players. The counter shows how many cards are left in the deck.

Gamblers sometimes had to protect themselves. The small weapon shown here is a rare Philadelphia Henry Deringer sold by Charles Curry in San Francisco between 1856 and 1863. RBCM 976.17.1-3; RBCM 981.141; RBCM 973.108.3; RBCM 2003.20.1

them and explore new ground, to inspire readers to rethink some of the clichés about the gold rush and gold-rush society.

The result is a collection of essays that offer different perspectives on the familiar stories and introduce new ways of examining the gold-rush years. They explore the legacies of the gold rush and the gold seekers who stayed on. The cultural makeup, the characteristics of being British Columbian were, for generations, reflective of the actions taken by gold seekers both during and after the rushes. Our pattern of urban distribution, our ideas of land usage and ownership, our established emphasis on resource extraction – forestry, mining and fishing – stretch back to the gold rush and to an attitude that saw this region as the fur-trading preserve of the Hudson's Bay Company or as a landscape of limitless opportunities for exploitation.

The first essay is not about British Columbia at all but the ancient indigenous metalworking tradition in what is now Colombia, South America. The authors – three curators at the Museo del Oro in Bogota – explain that indigenous peoples did not value gold for its own sake, but it was gold's properties of malleability that enabled it to be transformed through metalworking. For millennia before the Spanish arrived, goldsmiths crafted objects for use in social, political and religious rituals. Gold used in ornamentation expressed the power, status and cosmic vision of its wearers.

The existence of such gold works in Colombia inspired a 16th-century Spanish explorer to create the legend of *El Dorado* – a city of gold. European voyages of discovery in the Americas over successive centuries assumed the existence of other El Dorados. In 1858 British Columbia became, in popular parlance of the day, the *New El Dorado*. This first essay, therefore, situates British Columbia's gold rush in the western mythical idea of *El Dorado*. But more importantly the authors delineate the traditions and techniques of the goldsmiths. They describe the sophistication of the golden objects so created. We can see how Europeans encountering such a culture and "discovering" such works might be affected by gold fever, much in the same way 19th-century gold seekers travelled across the globe to British Columbia in search of nuggets and fortune.

This book includes two essays by Daniel Marshall. The first examines the actions of Governor James Douglas, who encouraged immigration to the colonies during the gold rush and specifically invited oppressed black Americans to come north. He intended that the Chinese and people of colour be considered equal under the law. He also wished to safeguard the rights of indigenous inhabitants into whose territories rushed the gold seekers, causing total disruption to their traditions and livelihood. Douglas's positions distinctly contradicted the American experience, and they confused the miners who had come from the California rush, where Chinese and First Nations rights were denied. Soon after Douglas retired, his successors overturned his policies and reinstated (without moderation) race-based assumptions of colonialism.

Curator Don Bourdon, an expert in historical photography, explains how artists and photographers responded to the landscape and the gold fields as they travelled along the Cariboo Wagon Road up the Fraser River to the Cariboo. Nineteenth-century sensibilities regarding the picturesque and the sublime inspired artists and photographers to create views of towns and miners within a common aesthetic of the contemporary viewing public. Illustrated newspapers of the day turned the photographs, sketches and watercolours of these artists into mass-media images through engraving and lithography, allowing them to be distributed widely and reprinted in following decades. Learning about photographers and artists who created representational images of towns, people and landscapes and then "reading" them as curated representations enables us to see beyond the content to their function as metaphor and as deliberately selected – cropped and framed – slices of "reality".

Educator Lily Chow has traced descendants of early Chinese gold seekers and interviewed them to uncover the family stories they have preserved over the generations. She has also examined government mining registers that sometimes provide the names of Chinese miners but more often list them in aggregate. She has uncovered small details showing that Chinese miners not only held mining claims but formed partnerships with non-Chinese people. Her essay demonstrates that teasing details from official records can lead to a new understanding about marginalized peoples in the gold rush, such as the Chinese.

History curator Tzu-I Chung follows this theme but focuses on material culture. She presents objects and artifacts held in museum collections as evidence of the Chinese miners and merchants who stayed and contributed to the establishment of permanent communities. She employs newspaper accounts, ship manifests and other records to reconstruct the important role that Chinese fraternal organizations played in connecting and supporting Chinese immigrants in Victoria and in small communities along the Fraser River. Chung emphasizes how these organizations established and maintained relationships between Chinese merchants and miners through their memberships, and how they provided economic and emotional support for miners, most of whom were young men with wives and children back in China.

Not all wives and children stayed home. Historian and photo-journalist Marie Elliott provides a preview of her larger project documenting and presenting information about women in the Cariboo during the years of the gold rush. Women are difficult to find in the historical record, often invisible as single dependants living at home and remaining so after marriage. There were very few settler women in the Cariboo. One miner noted in a letter home, "Oh I'm just sick of the faces of men."[8] Elliott has uncovered the identities of women previously unknown and ferreted out details about their lives, their entrepreneurial roles, their contributions to gold-rush society, and all too often their harsh ends.

Daniel Marshall's second essay encapsulates the central findings of his doctoral dissertation on the Fraser River War, later the subject of a documentary film. He discusses a little known series of horrific and violent events that unfolded over a few months in 1858. On the banks of the Fraser,

tensions escalated and turned ugly between the large contingent of American miners – fresh from the California diggings – and First Nations, many of whom also panned for gold. Outright war was just narrowly avoided. Marshall introduces the characters, provides the play-by-play and includes the actions of the First Nations – evidence gleaned from brief mentions in the historical records. This and Marshall's first essay challenge us to move beyond engrained narratives; they illustrate the value of small details and the importance of a wide net in the research process.

Jennifer Iredale draws on her 24 years of experience managing historic sites to discuss built heritage, specifically wooden buildings erected during BC's gold rushes, many of which survive today. She directs our attention to the often, modest scale and utilitarian nature of these buildings, and the techniques of construction and functionality in the communities or homesteads where they were erected. Some buildings have been preserved and are open to the public. Bridges and other public works, including, of course, the great Cariboo Wagon Road itself, are still visible in historical photographs and extant vestiges glimpsed from today's highway can be explored on foot.

Judy Campbell reflects on a career in heritage interpretation, of presenting the gold rush to tourist audiences and of the emotive qualities of place upon the presenter. A long-time employee and former chief executive officer of Barkerville Heritage Town, Campbell describes her emotional connections with heritage buildings, drawing in the essence of past personalities and patterns of living to gain a tacit understanding of history and to inform her own life and career decisions.[9] She introduces us to the importance of physical experience in learning about our past.

The gold rush formed defining life experiences for many who later ran for political office. This factor has not been accounted for in previous

Surveying instruments used by the Royal Engineers: an astronomical transit (left) used in the 1860s; and a two-day chronometer used in 1858 to establish BC's border with the United States along the 49th parallel.
RBCM 965.3003.1 a-d
RBCM 985.96.1 a-b

analyses of the lives and actions of these politicians. History curator Lorne Hammond reveals the social connections of Robert Carrall, the Cariboo's last representative in British Columbia's colonial legislature. Hammond shows how Carrall's life experiences contributed to his strong and steady campaign for BC to become a Canadian province. Carrall was a key member of a team of three men sent to Ottawa to negotiate the colony's entry into Confederation. Because extant personal records are few, his voice is not easily heard but Hammond's analysis of alternative sources enables us to learn about Carrall's undervalued contributions.

The people who came for the gold rush brought with them their cultures, languages and behaviours. They left legacies that flavour the character of today's British Columbia, including architectural styles, social organizations and networks, languages and customs. Their actions resonate today in place names, patterns of settlement and transportation corridors. The interactions of aboriginal and incoming groups resulted in dynamics that continue today in tensions about land ownership, usage, and resource exploitation. Our footsteps follow the literal and figurative pathways created and used by everyone who experienced the gold rush years in British Columbia. The essays in this book bring some of these pathways to light. ⚒

NOTES

1   "Far From Home", written by an unknown miner working at Emory's Bar on the Fraser River, was published in *Hutching's California Magazine* in September 1859 (p. 108).

2   Recent books include Marie Elliott's *Gold and Grand Dreams: Cariboo East in the Early Years* (Victoria: Horsdal and Schubart, 2000), Don Hauka's *Ned McGowan's War: The Birth of Modern British Columbia on the Fraser River Goldfields* (Vancouver: New Star Books, 2003), Mark Forsythe and Greg Dickson's *The Trail of 1858*, Medeira Park: Harbour Publishing, 2008), and Richard Wright's *Barkerville and the Cariboo Goldfields* (Victoria: Heritage House 2013).

3   Almost every gas station, grocery store and convenience store in the Fraser Canyon offers for sale a selection of local history books, many featuring accounts of the gold rush and personalities associated with it.

4   The earliest comprehensive settler census in 1881, several decades after the rush, shows a 7:3 ratio of males to females. See Jean Barman, *The West Beyond the West: A History of British Columbia* (Toronto: University of Toronto Press, 1991), p. 369 (chart). For the perspective of children in colonial BC, see Kathryn Bridge, "Being Young in the Country: Settler Children and Childhood in British Columbia and Alberta, 1860–1925". PhD dissertation, University of Victoria, 2012.

5   Some examples: Tina Loo's *Making Law, Order and Government Authority in British Columbia 1821–1871* (Toronto: University of Toronto Press, 1994); Adele Perry's *On the Edge of Empire: Gender, Race and the Making of British Columbia, 1849-1871* (UTP, 2001); Cole Harris's *The Resettlement of British Columbia* (Vancouver: University of British Columbia Press, 1997); and Jean Barman's *French Canadians, Furs and Indigenous Women in the Making of the Pacific Northwest* (UBCP, 2014).

6   Estimates for the native population in the southern Strait of Georgia and Fraser River to Lytton is at least 50,000 (a huge decline after smallpox and other diseases) supporting more than 100 winter villages (Harris, pp. 24, 25, 30).

7   James Teit lived in Spences Bridge, married to a Nlaka'pamux woman. Beginning in the 1890s he worked for anthropologist Franz Boas. For further information see *Traditions of the Thompson River Indians of British Columbia*, collected and annotated by James Teit, with an introduction by Franz Boas (Houghton Mifflin, 1898) and *Publications of the Jesup North Pacific Expedition* (New York: American Museum of Natural History, 1898-1903.

8   Adele Perry, "Oh I'm Just Sick of the Faces of Men": Gender Imbalance, Race, Sexuality, and Sociability" *BC Studies*, University of British Columbia, 1995, No 105/106.

9   For more information on the tacit and the tactile in historical discovery see Joy Parr, "Notes for a More Sensuous History of Twentieth-Century Canada: The Timely, the Tacit, and the Material Body," *The Canadian Historical Review* 82, no. 4 (2001).

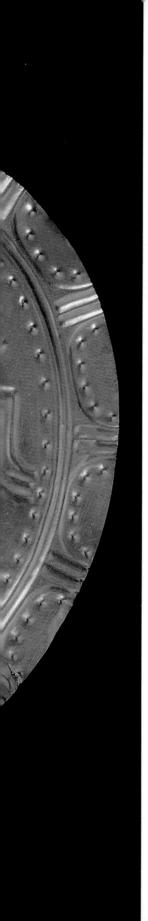

Pre-Hispanic Metalwork of Colombia

María Alicia Uribe Villegas, Juan Pablo Quintero
Guzmán and Héctor García Botero

IIIIIIIIIIIIIIIIIIIIIIIIIIIIIIIIIIIIIIIIIIIIIIIIII

DIVERSE COLOMBIA

COLOMBIA IS A LAND of geographical and cultural diversity. It is the most northerly country in South America and benefits from having coastlines on both the Pacific and the Caribbean. Located in the inter-tropical zone, Colombia is divided into five main natural regions, each boasting a variety of relief, climates and ecosystems. The hot Amazon rainforest in the south is in marked contrast to the vast Orinoco grasslands in the east. The Andes range in the west is split into three branches, where the mountain landscape results in intermediate and cold climates, while the narrow alluvial plain that runs along the Pacific coast is covered with tropical rainforest and an intricate maze of mangrove swamps. In the north the Caribbean region is a combination of beaches, deserts, burning-hot plains, rainforest and, on the Sierra Nevada de Santa Marta, the highest peaks in all Colombia, which rise to 5775 metres above sea level.

The country's cultural diversity is the result of its long and complex history. The land has been inhabited for more than 15,000 years by groups with widely differing ways of life. Indigenous societies in the pre-Hispanic past developed their own subsistence methods, were in contact with each other and engaged in cultural exchanges. After the Spaniards reached the coasts of Colombia, around 1500, European culture was imposed in much of the country, although many traditional indigenous groups and practices managed to adapt and have survived to the present day. There are 102 indigenous groups in Colombia today, speaking 64 languages. After the Conquest and throughout the 300 years of the colonial era, the trafficking of African slaves, imported to labour in the mines and on the large estates, resulted in further additions to the cultural panorama. And this diversity was nourished even further in the 19th and 20th centuries by the arrival of migrants from the Near East, Asia and Europe.

THE PRE-HISPANIC METALWORK OF COLOMBIA

SOUTH AMERICAN METALLURGY originated in Peru about 4000 years ago and later spread to Colombia. Groups with notable skills in the working of metals were living in Tumaco, in the Pacific region, by the 5th century BCE. From then until the time of the Spanish Conquest – a period of almost two thousand years –the land today known as Colombia saw a multitude of developments in metallurgy and metalworking styles, thousands of objects made, and complex techniques perfected.

Much pre-Hispanic metalwork was produced in chieftainships, which often occupied a valley or wider expanse of territory and brought various communities together around a permanent leader. Some, such as the Muisca and Zenú chieftainships, were very large and controlled several thousand hectares of land and hundreds of thousands of people. They were hierarchical societies where the power and status of the elite were based, to a large extent, on their sacred links with the gods and their control of rituals and the trading of prestige goods over great distances. At the top of the social pyramid was the principal chieftain, who lesser leaders answered to, and under these latter were lower-ranking figures. Chieftains enjoyed vast privileges, including control over luxury goods such as metalwork.

The prosperous economy resulted in significant surpluses, and these were used to support specialists – including metalsmiths, as well as religious and political leaders – in busy trading activities and in the building of labour-intensive infrastructure works. Many chieftainship societies engaged in intensive agriculture based around the growing of corn (*Zea mays*) or cassava (*Manihot* sp.). In some cases, the elites also controlled economic resources such as salt, gold mines and coca plantations, or they had a group of traders at their disposal, which enabled them to gain access to products and goods from distant regions.

As in the rest of the Americas, ancient metallurgy in Colombia can be viewed as a communication technology that concentrated on producing objects which expressed and formed status, power and visions of the cosmos. The contexts in which pre-Hispanic metalwork was used, considered alongside the material properties of the objects and their manufacturing technique and iconography, help us to understand the meanings of the objects.

The funerary practices of certain pre-Hispanic societies included burying metal objects with the deceased, to accompany them on their journey to the great beyond. Their bodies were covered with ornaments such as masks and breastplates. Some examples of funerary attire included artifacts with a profound cosmological significance, such as lime containers made in the form of a woman or a calabash, possibly associated with the person's social position and specialist work. Ornaments that had been intentionally broken, twisted, struck or punctured have been found in some graves, seemingly indicating that they had been required to die along with their owner.

Some pre-Hispanic societies also used metal objects in offerings. In addition to metal, objects were made from other materials (some have survived to this day and other have disappeared because of environmental factors). As a context, offerings included, besides the material culture, the spiritual being it was addressed to, the message it contained, the place where it was offered up, the rite, the person making the offering and the officiating priest.

One of the most widespread uses of metalwork was for ornaments that served as status symbols or emblems in the social group. The scarcity or abundance of these objects, as well as the simplicity or complexity of their iconography, may be related to whether their use was restricted or extensive among the population. In some societies, ornaments served as a medium for transforming the leaders, who, based on their profound knowledge of the cosmos, could transmute into bats, jaguars or other creatures in order to take on their powers by wearing them.

Some items of ritual paraphernalia, such as metal *poporos* (lime containers), trays and spoons, were used in specific ceremonies connected with the preparing and consuming of sacred and wisdom-granting plants which stimulated the person and enabled him to communicate with spiritual beings.

THE METALS USED AND THEIR PROPERTIES

FOUR METALS WERE USED IN COLOMBIA in pre-Hispanic times: gold, copper, silver and platinum. Gold and copper were the ones used most frequently, and they were often mixed together to form alloys that scholars refer to as *tumbaga*, which acquired different properties than those of their component metals. Gold came mostly from alluvial deposits in the rivers that flow down from the central and western cordilleras, and was obtained by panning (washing the sands in wooden pans) and sometimes with the help of canals to divert the water. Shafts were also sunk so that the metal could be mined from seams, such as in the Buriticá region in Antioquia or in Marmato, Caldas. Gold was used in its natural state, without refining and complete with all its impurities – mostly silver, but also platinum and other similar metals in some regions. We know little about the origin of the copper, which seemingly came from natural deposits and also from the processing of ores.

Platinum, a metal that melts at a very high temperature, beyond the reach of pre-Hispanic technology, was used by Tumaco-La Tolita metalsmiths in the Pacific region, who extracted it from rivers and mixed it with gold. This mixture, when heated to the melting point of gold trapped the platinum within the gold. The material, which had taken on a silvery colour, could then be worked and shaped by the metalsmith.

Silver was used as a raw material for making artifacts only on the high plains of Nariño, in southern Colombia. This region was strongly influenced by people from the southern Andes, where this metal was used widely.

Just as elsewhere in pre-Hispanic America, metallurgists in Colombia concentrated on making objects associated with religion, their vision of the cosmos, political power and social organization. It was these spheres – rather than war, the economy or transport, as seen in various parts of Europe and Asia in ancient times – that were the driving force behind metallurgical developments in the New World. Unlike the way in which gold and other precious metals today acquire meaning through their economic value and because they represent a means of accumulating material wealth, indigenous societies believed that objects made from these metals had religious, spiritual and symbolic connotations. Metal objects transmitted ideas not just through the forms depicted or their iconography but also through their materials, the manufacturing and casting techniques used, and their sensory properties, such as colour, shine and sound. Thus gold was not seen to be a valuable material; it acquired a value only when it was transformed into a cultural object.

Colour has been considered one of the decisive factors in the development of ancient American metallurgy, and this was unquestionably true in the case of various metalwork styles in Colombia. The different colours of metals and their alloys had distinct symbolic connotations and were attributed with having particular powers and properties that were transmitted to the respective objects and, through them, to whoever used them. Various techniques were developed for manipulating colour, whether it was the actual metals that were chosen (in some cases, such as native gold, they contained impurities that gave them varying shades), the different proportions in which they were mixed to form alloys, or the use of surface gilding or scraping techniques. Combining different metals on a single object, or combining metal with other materials such as stone, shell or organic elements, also helped to create colour effects.

Shine was another vital property in Colombian metallurgy. As with colour, it encouraged the development of various techniques, as well as new forms, shapes and decorations. Polishing and burnishing techniques using stone, sand and other materials achieved shines of different intensities, while acids were used to create matte surfaces that contrasted with shiny ones in attractive designs. Hanging plates, which were a feature of virtually all metalwork styles, made objects sparkle.

Certain sounds were also produced by carefully selecting manufacturing techniques and materials, and also because of the particular shape of the object. Bells and rattles are found in several Colombian metalwork styles, as are trumpets and Pan's pipes. Identical examples of the latter were made in tumbaga and in silver and gold alloys. Hanging plates could also have been important because of the sound they made.

METALWORK TECHNIQUES

COLOMBIAN METALLURGICAL TECHNOLOGY is highly complex and diverse. Pre-Hispanic metalsmiths were masters not only of different metals and alloys but also of manufacturing techniques like hammering and variations on the process of casting using the lost wax method. They employed various types of surface gilding and polishing, used granulation and heat welding as well as embossing techniques, and knew various ways of assembling and repairing objects. Several of these processes might be involved in producing an object, which proves that a metalsmith required vast knowledge and extensive skills. In addition to a detailed knowledge of metalworking techniques, he had to be skilled in working with wax, clay, and probably also the stone, shell and horn that were used for making tools or the cores of objects. An expert management of fire, temperature and atmosphere was fundamental. We do not know whether any kind of differentiation was made between specialists who used the various materials and techniques, or whether a metalsmith had to master all (or the vast majority of them). And as with all activities in indigenous life, metallurgy had an immaterial dimension: metals, wax, tools and techniques all had symbolic and spiritual meanings, and metalworking involved engaging in a series of rituals.

HAMMERING AND EMBOSSING

METALSMITHS STRUCK CASTINGS against slabs or stone anvils to make sheets. Depending on the alloy, the dimensions of the object or the phase of the work, hammers of different materials and of differing shapes, sizes and weights were used. Stone slabs and polishers smoothed the sheets and made surfaces and thicknesses that were uniform. Metal becomes brittle and tends to fracture when it is hammered; therefore had to be heated until it was red-hot and then cooled by immersing it in water. This process, called annealing, enables the sheet to go on being struck until the desired size and thickness are obtained.

Chisels made of stone or tumbaga, which is a hard, resistant alloy, were used for marking sheets and cutting them into the final shape of the object.

Decorative designs were sketched on the back with burins, after which the motif was pressed and brought out on both surfaces with the help of chisels and punches while the object was resting on soft, firm materials or on forms carved previously from some other hard material. Three-dimensional objects were made by assembling various sheets using nails, stitches or flanges, or by heating and applying pressure, sometimes on clay, wood or shell models.

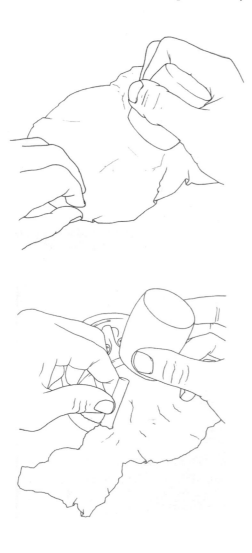

Shaping annealed metal.

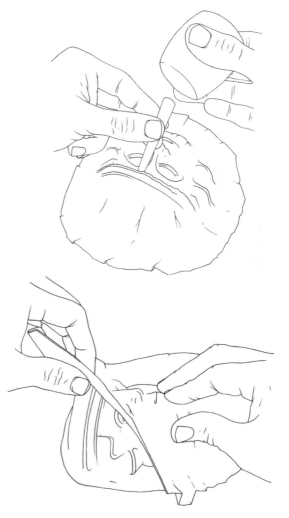

Sketching and shaping motifs.

CASTING USING THE LOST WAX TECHNIQUE

PRE-HISPANIC METALSMITHS in the area today known as Colombia made important developments and innovations in casting techniques and became considerably skilled in what is known as the lost wax method. This technique differentiates Colombian metallurgy from that found elsewhere in pre-Hispanic America.

The process of producing a cast object involved first making a model of it, complete with all details, out of a soft, highly malleable wax from a type of stingless bee (*Tetragonisca angustula*). The metalsmith added a wax funnel and feeder channels through which the metal would flow, and then applied a fine layer of ground charcoal and liquid clay to the whole surface. The mould was made by covering this model with a porous clay, leaving an opening where the funnel was located. The metalsmith heated the mould to harden it and to drain the melted wax from inside it. He then poured molten metal into the hot mould. After it cooled, the mould could be broken to extract the object. The object was generally finished by cutting off excess parts (the funnel and feeder channels) and then polished or subjected to a surface gilding process. Because the lost wax method requires the mould to be broken, every object made this way was unique.

A variation on this method, namely casting using the lost wax technique with a core, was used for making hollow three-dimensional objects. The metalsmith first modelled the figures or containers in clay and charcoal. He then covered this core with wax and modelled the designs to be added on the outside of the object. He added a number of partitions, linking the core to the mould, in order to keep the core in place when the wax was removed. From that point on, the metalsmith followed the basic process in the lost wax method. The holes left by the partitions were filled in with plugs of the same metal at the end.

Muisca metalsmiths used slate matrices to stamp designs on small wax sheets, and these were then reproduced in metal using the lost wax technique.

MULTIPLE CASTINGS

METALSMITHS produced jointed or multicoloured objects by casting in various stages, using alloys with ever lower fusion points. Twin-metal lime sticks like these, which are unique in America, come from Valle del Cauca.

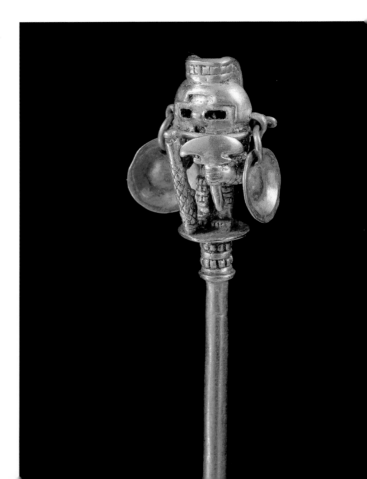

Limestick used in ritual ceremonies. Calima-Yotoco Period, 200 BCE – 1300 CE. Museo del Oro O05234

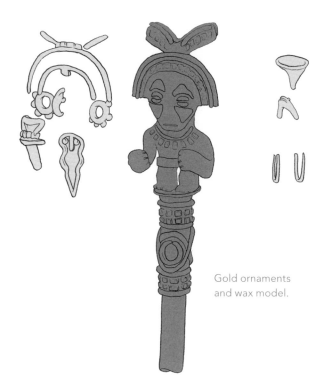

Gold ornaments and wax model.

Metal ornaments joined to the wax model.

The first step consisted of making the ornaments for the stick separately, out of gold or a gold-rich alloy, using the lost wax technique. The metal ornaments were then joined to the wax model with the anthropomorphous figure of the stick, after which both the wax model and the ornaments were coated with a clay mould, and the tumbaga alloy – which had a lower fusion temperature than that of the ornaments – was poured. When the mould was cold, it had to be broken in order to extract the metal object.

Limestick used in ritual ceremonies. Calima-Yotoco Period, 200 BCE – 1300 CE. Museo del Oro O07534

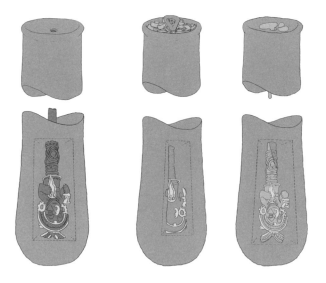
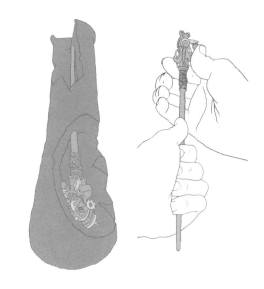

Pouring the tumbaga alloy into the clay mould.

Breaking the mould to reveal the lime stick.

DEPLETION GILDING

VARIOUS COLOMBIAN METALWORK STYLES used depletion gilding as a technique for enriching the gold on the surface of tumbaga objects in order to produce a gilded surface layer. Or, by partly scraping it, a metalsmith could create designs in contrasting colours, ranging from the yellow of the surface to the reddish hue of the core. Various chemical processes were involved in this technique. By heating the object, the metalsmith oxidized the copper on the surface, and he then cleaned the oxides with vegetable acid solutions, such as those produced by Sheep Sorrel (*Oxalis pubescens*). If this process was repeated several times, a surface layer rich in gold was created. This got worn away with use and left the base alloy visible. Nariño metalsmiths created geometric designs in different colours by scraping the gold surface to reveal the red underneath.

METALWORKING SOCIETIES

METALWORK WAS PRODUCED over a wide area of the country in pre-Hispanic times, in the Andean, Caribbean and Pacific regions. Archaeologists have defined 12 metalworking areas in Colombia where important styles developed: in the Caribbean region are the Tairona, Zenú and Urabá areas; in the Andean region the Quimbaya, Muisca, Tolima, Calima-Malagana, San Agustín, Tierradentro, Cauca and Nariño areas; and in the Pacific region the Tumaco-La Tolita area, which extends into Ecuador. Metallurgy existed in most of these areas from the early years of the Christian era, and production continued without interruption until the time of the Spanish Conquest – although major changes in metalworking styles occurred in some regions over the course of time, with sophisticated technological developments and innovations.

Archaeological Regions and Current Indigenous Groups

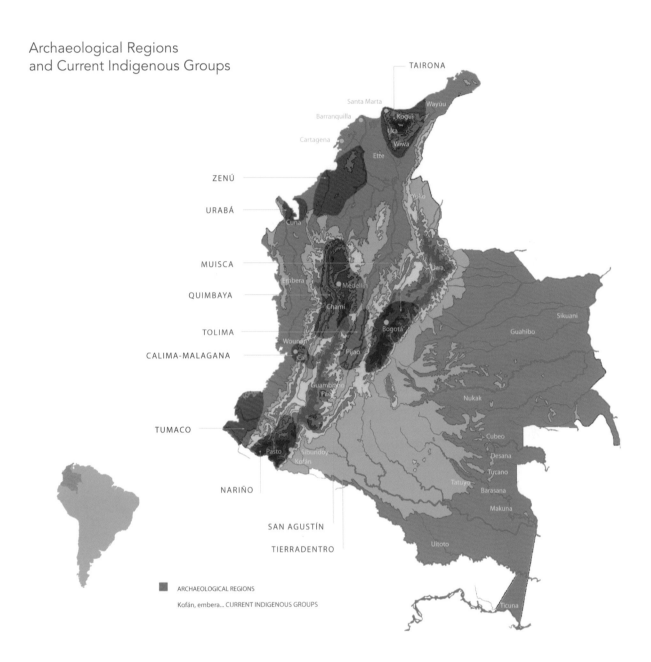

TAIRONA

Santa Marta

Barranquilla

Cartagena

Wayúu

Kogui

Ijka

Wiwa

Ette

ZENÚ

URABÁ

Cuna

Yuko

MUISCA

Embera

Uwa

Medellín

QUIMBAYA

Chamí

Sikuani

Bogotá

Guahibo

TOLIMA

CALIMA-MALAGANA

Wounán

Cali

Pijao

Guambiano

Páez

Nukak

Cubeo

TUMACO

Desana

Pasto

Sibundoy

Kofán

Tucano

Tatuyo

Barasana

Makuna

NARIÑO

SAN AGUSTÍN

TIERRADENTRO

Uitoto

Ticuna

◼ ARCHAEOLOGICAL REGIONS

Kofán, embera... CURRENT INDIGENOUS GROUPS

The regional differences in Colombian metalwork styles relate to the materials and techniques employed, the shapes and iconography of the objects, and the objects' uses and meanings. These differences tell us about sociocultural processes and particular cultural identities.

But clear similarities also exist between several of the styles in some regions and during certain periods, and this, in turn, tells us about the relationships and connections that existed between societies.

Chronology of the Goldworking Societies

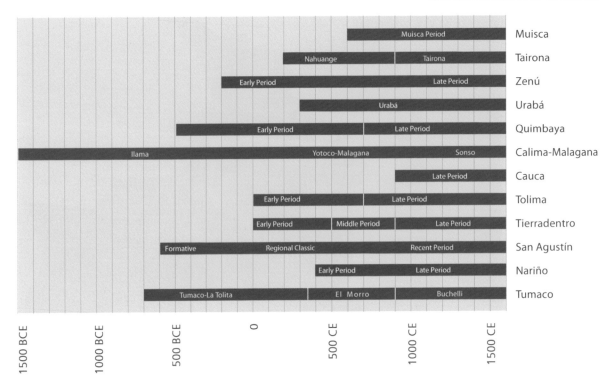

Region			
Muisca Period			Muisca
Nahuange / Tairona			Tairona
Early Period / Late Period			Zenú
Urabá			Urabá
Early Period / Late Period			Quimbaya
Ilama / Yotoco-Malagana / Sonso			Calima-Malagana
Late Period			Cauca
Early Period / Late Period			Tolima
Early Period / Middle Period / Late Period			Tierradentro
Formative / Regional Classic / Recent Period			San Agustín
Early Period / Late Period			Nariño
Tumaco-La Tolita / El Morro / Buchelli			Tumaco

1500 BCE — 1000 BCE — 500 BCE — 0 — 500 CE — 1000 CE — 1500 CE

TUMACO

THE PACIFIC COASTAL PLAIN, from the mangrove swamps to the tropical forests of the Andean foothills, offered pre-Hispanic societies a wide range of biological and mineral resources. Their pottery depicts sumptuous chieftains and leading members of the ordinary public, even sick and deformed persons. These clay figures illustrate ornaments typical of Tumaco metal art, which is the oldest in Colombia (5th century BC): small nose rings and earrings made from numerous parts joined together by granulation and applications of different shapes that were to be inserted into the skin. Metalsmiths developed ingenious techniques for working platinum combined with gold.

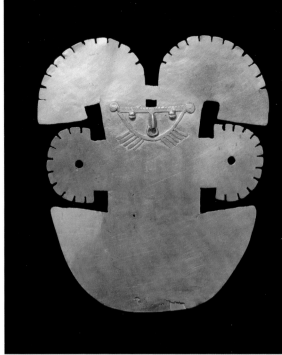

Pectoral. Calima Valle – Malagana Period, 200 BCE – 1300 CE. Museo del Oro O03682

Breastplate. Calima Valle – Sonso Period, 650 BCE – 1600 CE. Museo del Oro O01221

CALIMA-MALAGANA

THE EARLIEST EVIDENCE OF SEDENTARY FARMERS in the Calima region, on the western cordillera, dates from 1500 BCE. During the Ilama Period (15th century BCE to 1st century CE), these groups of excellent potters began to make gold objects. Later, in the Yotoco Period (2nd to 13th centuries CE), the population spread and occupied valleys and hills, altering the landscape with drainage channels, crop-growing plots, and terracing for houses and paths. Their metalsmiths produced splendid objects, such as attractive apparel consisting of large diadems, nose rings and breastplates. During the Sonso Period (11th to 16th centuries CE), metalwork typically consisted of smaller, simpler objects and became less important as a symbol of hierarchy. People living in the Malagana region in the Cauca valley were closely linked to those of Calima and so their cultural works were similar.

SAN AGUSTÍN

IN THE MOUNTAINOUS REGION OF SAN AGUSTÍN, deep in the Colombian massif where the Andean cordillera splits into two branches and where the Cauca and Magdalena rivers rise, impressive statues made of volcanic stone are clear evidence of the time when a hierarchical society was at its height, in the Regional Classical Period (1st to 10th centuries CE). Its leaders were buried in artificial mounds watched over by these statues with features of jaguars, birds of prey, snakes or aggressive warriors. Occasionally the buried leaders were accompanied by metal ornaments: simple, stylized breastplates, diadems, earrings and necklaces. In the Recent Period (10th to 16th centuries CE), by which time the population had grown, political power was based on economic rather than symbolic matters.

Facing page: Anthropomorphous figure with intentional altered skull. Pacific Coast – Inguapí Period, 700 BC – 350 AD. Museo del Oro C09604

TIERRADENTRO

SPANIARDS GAVE THE NAME TIERRADENTRO to the eastern flanks of the central cordillera, in Cauca province, because of the rugged terrain. During the Middle Period (5th to 9th centuries CE), the inhabitants carved deep graves with spiral staircases and underground chambers out of the volcanic tufa, and painted them with red and black geometric figures to conjure up images of their homes. Tierradentro metal masks, earrings and breastplates were sometimes embossed with jaguar figures similar to those on the statues at San Agustín.

CAUCA

SOMETIME BETWEEN the 10th and 16th centuries CE, metalsmiths in the upper Cauca valley in the area around Popayán and the central cordillera produced a group of objects rich in mythological iconography: large breastplates with impressive bird-man figures and ornaments depicting fantastic animals that were a combination of mammals, frogs and birds. Around the time of the Conquest, the region was inhabited by farming groups scattered over the plains and the slopes of the mountains. The pottery and gold funerary attire in their graves reflects a strict social hierarchy.

NARIÑO

THE COLD ANDEAN HIGH PLAINS around the frontier between Colombia and Ecuador were inhabited from the 5th century CE onwards by various ethnic groups. Their metalsmiths used particular techniques to manufacture a group of objects with designs that were unique: diadems, nose rings, breastplates, ear pendants and rotating

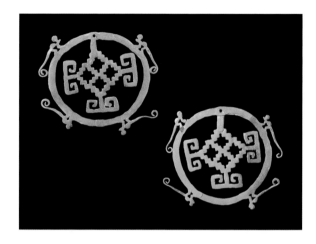

Pendent earrings. Nariño Plateau – Late Period, 600 AD – 1700 AD. Museo del Oro O25405-06

Pectoral in the form of a bird-man with zoomorphous figures. Upper Cauca – Late Period, 900 AD – 1600AD. Museo del Oro O06414

discs with geometric shapes and decorations that were a combination of openwork, colours and textures. They also worked silver, which was a feature of the southern Andes. Their leaders were buried in graves up to 40 metres deep.

TOLIMA

THE VALLEY OF THE MAGDALENA, Colombia's most important river, was significant in pre-Hispanic times in terms of population movements and the bartering of goods. Metalwork with an abstract, symmetrical and schematic style was typical of the art produced in this area from the beginning of the Common Era, often depicting human figures with wings and jaguar jaws, as well as fabulous insects. When Spaniards arrived, the area was inhabited by groups of farmers, gatherers and fishermen, who produced simple metalwork.

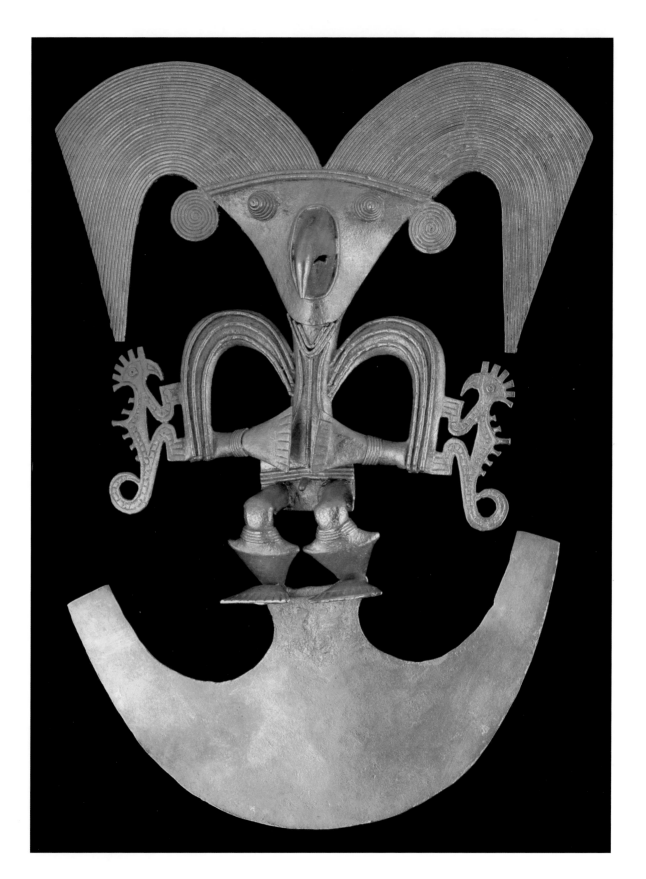

Left: Pectoral in the form of a jaguar-man. Tolima Region – Middle Tolima Period, 1 CE – 700 CE. Museo del Oro O06336

Right: Phitomorphous Lime Container, or poporo. Middle Cauca – Early Quimbaya Period, 500 BCE – 700 CE. Museo del Oro O02995

QUIMBAYA

METALSMITHS in the mid Cauca valley and canyon in the Early Period (5th century BCE to 7th century CE) made outstanding metal *poporos*, containers for storing the lime that was used with coca leaves, in realistic shapes of humans or fruit. Quimbayan metalsmiths developed extraordinary skills in casting tumbaga alloys using the lost wax technique with core. These were farming and mining communities where the leaders enjoyed the privilege of using metal and its symbolic powers. During the Late Period (7th to 16th centuries CE) the use of metalwork spread to a wider spectrum of the population, and flat, geometric and hammered ornaments were produced. The conquistadors encountered a dense population in this region, who withstood the invasion of their territory in a warrior-like and symbolic manner.

ZENÚ

THE CARIBBEAN TROPICAL PLAINS are an area of marshes, estuaries and grasslands. The Zenúes had spread across the basins of the Sinú, San Jorge, Cauca and Nechí rivers several centuries before the Christian era, and their water management schemes in floodable areas consisted of a system of canals and artificial platforms covering about 700,000 hectares. At their height, in the first millennium of the Common Era, their chiefs were buried in tombs under large mounds of earth, wearing funerary attire that included large, heavy metal breastplates, nose rings and staff heads.

Nose ring. Caribbean Plains – Zenú Tradition, 200 BCE – 1000 CE. Museo del Oro O33133

The Zenú population started to decline around 1200 CE. Part of their territory, and also the San Jacinto Range, was occupied by other groups of fishermen, metalsmiths and farmers that the Spaniards referred to as Malibúes. Although Malibú metalwork had similar features to that of the Zenúes, it differed in that the Malibúes used copper-rich alloys to make ornaments shaped like cats, birds and schematized humans with the bodies of fish, lizards or crustaceans.

URABÁ

BECAUSE OF ITS STRATEGIC LOCATION at the base of the Isthmus of Panama – a point of entry into South America – its closeness to two oceans and its ease of access to the interior, the Urabá region has been a land of convergence and exchange since ancient times. Urabá metalwork reflects Urabá's links with the isthmus, the Caribbean, and the Cauca basin. Spiral breastplates, pendants in the shape of a double bird, ornaments shaped like animals with raised tails, and realistic human figures are common here and in these other areas.

TAIRONA

THE COASTAL BAYS at the foot of the Sierra Nevada de Santa Marta were inhabited during the Nahuange Period (2nd to 10th centuries CE) by pottery-making societies who engaged in fishing, salt extraction and farming. Their metalsmiths manufactured realistic female and zoomorphous tumbaga ornaments with geometric shapes. In the Tairona Period (10th to 16th centuries CE), they settled on the mountainsides of the Sierra Nevada and built stone cities, water systems and pathways which are the most important pre-Hispanic engineering works in Colombia. Casting using

Pendant in form of a Bat-Man. Sierra Nevada de Santa Marta – Tairona Period, 900 CE – 1600 CE. Museo del Oro O11795

the lost wax technique with core became popular, as did depletion gilding. And bat and bat-man iconography came to predominate.

MUISCA

THE MUISCAS POPULATED the high plains of Colombia's central cordillera around the 7th century CE. They were farmers who grew corn, potatoes and other Andean tubers, and they lived in communities scattered on the mountainsides and in the valleys that were ruled over by chieftains. The people gathered periodically at ceremonial centres to perform rituals in which gold played a fundamental role. They made metal body ornaments and votive figures, or *tunjos*, by casting using the lost wax technique in tumbaga alloys, and these had a rough surface finish. *Tunjos*, which were small figures depicting human beings, animals and scenes from political and social life, were deposited as offerings on hills and in caves, shrines and sacred lakes.

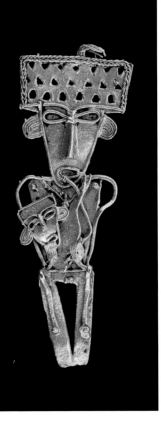

Anthropomorfous votive figure, known as tunjo. Eastern Cordillera – Muisca Period, 600 CE – 1600 CE. Museo del Oro O28695

AFTER THE CONQUEST

THE VAST, UNEXPLORED SOUTH AMERICAN CONTI-NENT was seen by Europeans as a possible source of the fantastic beings and places, as the minds of the 15th-century European navigators were full of the news of cities of gold and inexhaustible sources of spices, pearls and other riches mentioned in ancient travellers' tales. Finding the wonderful place where gold never ran out was a fundamental objective of various expeditions that were organized to penetrate the New World, the territory today known as Colombia in particular.

It was during the expansion period in the 16th century that the name El Dorado was coined, to refer to an unlimited source of gold somewhere on the continent of America. The name brought together in a single expression two different European ideas: El Dorado the city and El Dorado the person. In the former sense it referred to Manoa, a city of gold like the cities with gold castles in the Far East mentioned by Marco Polo. Expeditions that set out to find the city resulted in confrontations with the Incas and European discovery of the Amazon River. The idea of El Dorado as a person arose from the way in which the Europeans interpreted and recorded news they received from indigenous groups about a certain ceremony. In this ceremony, a chieftain with his body covered in gold dust was carried on a raft to the centre of a great lake, where he threw offerings of gold, emeralds and other materials into the water while other participants did the same from shore. It was because they were following up on these rumours that the expeditions led by Gonzalo Jiménez de Quesada, Nicolás de Federmann and Sebastián de Belalcázar met on the high plains of Cundinamarca and Boyacá, where the former founded the city of Bogotá, the present-day capital of Colombia.

Several of the earliest European settlements in what is today known as Colombia were established near sources of gold and were named accordingly. Examples include the Castilla de Oro provincial government, one of the first names given to the region in the northern part of Colombia, and Rio de Oro, one of the early Spanish towns near a gold deposit on the eastern cordillera. Although many of these early settlements had a short life, others came to be the forerunners of more permanent towns. The settlements were centres of gold mining operations, and from them commercial, political and economic relations were established with indigenous peoples.

Mobilizing the indigenous population was crucial to gold mining activities. Whole settlements and individual people were relocated so that production demands could be met. Some are known to have come from as far away as Peru, and it was from them that the natives learned how to mine gold, because it was not part of their traditional knowledge. Although it is believed to have been a process involving much physical violence, the Spaniards were forced to act differently in Nueva Granada. Violence was particularly useless with indigenous communities who were not organized in chieftainships, because they simply fled from any Spanish excesses, taking refuge outside the limits of the territory that was under European control. In the case of chieftainships, like the Muiscas on the high plains of Cundinamarca and

Boyacá, the Spaniards established relationships and forged alliances directly with the chieftains, who cooperated by making their people available to the Spaniards, who then organized the gold-mining labour squads. In exchange the chieftains remained in control of their subjects.

The conflict over gold revolved around differing valuations placed on the metal. These opposing views became apparent when metal objects were being assessed, while the conquistadors valued them for the metal they contained, which could be recovered by melting the objects down, the natives valued the material and symbolic work of the metalsmith, and the use of the objects in specific cultural contexts, such as offerings, burials or ritual celebrations. The Europeans' greed for more and more metal disconcerted the natives. In his *Historia General de las Indias*, Francisco López de Gómara recorded an indigenous man called Panquiaco addressing the Spaniards in the following terms:

> If I knew, Christians, that you were going to quarrel over my gold, I wouldn't give it to you, because I'm a friend of peace and harmony. I'm amazed at your blindness and madness, that you break up such well-worked jewels to make sticks out of them, and that being such fiends, you fight over so little. You'd be better off in your own land, which is so far away from here, if the people there are as wise and refined as you claim, and not come to fight where you don't belong, where we rude and barbaric men, as you call us, live happily. But if you're so desperate for gold that you even kill those who have it, I will show you a land where you will get sick and tired of it.[1]

Metal objects were confiscated as part of the European evangelization campaign, which condemned indigenous spiritual practices as idolatry or forms of devil worship. Since metal objects played a fundamental role in ceremonies, offerings and ritual attire, the Spaniards saw in them a concrete way to attack native spirituality. And it was not just metalwork worn by the living that was confiscated, because in northern Colombia indigenous graves, referred to as "burials of the devil", were plundered on a large scale – so much so that the amount of metal removed from graves led to notable inflation in the recently-founded city of Cartagena de Indias in the middle of the 16th century. The banning and persecution of indigenous beliefs was reinforced by controlling and condemning the production of and trafficking in metal objects.

Indigenous societies and their metalwork practices have been transformed by constant exchanges with other societies. As Spanish rule was consolidated, and now during the republican era, pre-Hispanic metallurgy traditions have gradually been transformed from the work of indigenous descendants in colonial silverwork to the introduction of hitherto unknown metals and labour technology, new knowledge and practices have emerged in the country. While metalwork production has disappeared completely in some regions, it has been transformed in areas where it has been combined with African and European techniques. These traditions are still alive today in towns like Santa Fe de Antioquia, Mompox and Barbacoas. And while new works in new traditions are being made, various present-day indigenous groups still possess metal objects that have been handed down from their ancestors and preserve, in their mythologies, stories about the meaning of gold. ⚒

NOTES

1   Francisco López de Gómara. *Historia General de las Indias y Vida de Hernán Cortés* (originally published in 1553). Caracas: Biblioteca Ayacucho, 1979, p. 133.

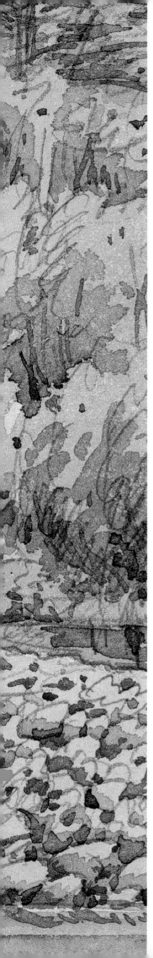

The British Columbia Commonwealth

Gold Seekers and the Rush for Freedom

Daniel Marshall

||||||||||||||||||||||||||||||||||||||||||||||||||

THE 1858 BRITISH COLUMBIA GOLD RUSH is a transnational story very much like California's 1849 gold rush, yet it's decidedly different for having provided a comparatively safe haven for persecuted minorities and protecting indigenous peoples. In the world history of gold rushes, this safe haven is a largely untold story.

The Hudson's Bay Company (HBC) had a longstanding partnership with indigenous peoples, and this historic, pre-1858 fur-trade partnership between First Nations and Europeans – imbued with the traditions of Liberal humanitarianism, whereby an ethic of kindness, benevolence and sympathy were extended universally and impartially to all human beings – ultimately confronted the harshest attitudes and elements of these gold-rush manias. In doing so, the HBC offered freedom for all under British law.

This was certainly not the case in the United States. Imagine for a moment you were an indigenous person driven into submission by the US Army and concentrated in large reservations – a relocation outside ancient, traditional territories. Or what if you were a black American parent living in California whose young daughter was assaulted by a white American miner, with no legal recourse as a consequence of black testimony being inadmissible in courts of law? And how would you feel as a high-ranking HBC official partnered with an indigenous woman if your mixed-blood children were disenfranchised – their rights stripped – in their own home territory of southern "Old Oregon" (Washington, Oregon and Idaho)? These imaginings actually happened yet remain, for the most part, also untold.

Chinese Gold Washers on the Fraser River, about 1864. William G.R. Hind, oil on card. McCord Museum N-0000.68.1

Before the establishment of the Oregon Boundary Settlement of 1846 (by which Britain and the United States extended the 49th parallel westward to the Pacific Slope as the international divide), there had existed a period of joint British-American sovereignty on the Northwest Coast in which Old Oregon was born – that is, the period when American pioneers went west to claim lands already occupied by the HBC, let alone the First Nations who had lived on these lands since time immemorial. James Douglas, the future governor of British Columbia, was himself of mixed-blood (Scottish and West Indian) and had experienced firsthand the growing racist, exclusionary policies adopted in Old Oregon, particularly after 1843.[1] The Americans on the Oregon Trail not only brought their wagons loaded with the necessities required for a fresh start – the residual trappings of the civilization they left behind – but also the insular prejudices for which they were generally known.

As historian John C. Jackson has noted of the influx of Americans, "Most early overlanders came from communities that feared and firmly repudiated racial intermarriage, believing it a threat to frontier survival."[2] In short order, the Oregon Provisional Government began passing exclusionary laws, rules and regulations. Most HBC mixed-blood families, like the Douglas family, were forced to move north to Fort Victoria (established in 1843), to escape legislation that effectively disenfranchised the mixed-blood children of fur-trade unions – "the custom of the country" as it was known.

Further American immigration in 1845 "brought in a voting bloc that seized control of the legislature and made laws for its own benefit".[3] Douglas's predecessor, Chief Factor John McLoughlin (the "Father of Oregon"), wrote of the changing circumstances brought by these American squatters from the east, imbued with notions of Manifest Destiny:

Sir James Douglas, 1864. BCA A-01228

It is reported that some of the immigrants last come have said that every man who has an Indian wife ought to be driven out of the country, and that the half-breeds should not be allowed to hold lands. This report was communicated to the Canadians by one of the American trappers who has an Indian wife, and excited great sensation among the Americans and Canadians who have half-breed families. But the persons accused of suggesting this measure deny it, but others say still it is true, and one of the American trappers believes it so firmly, that he bought powder and ball to prepare himself to resist.[4]

By 1862 Oregon adopted a law that required all blacks, Chinese, Hawaiians and mixed-bloods residing in the state to pay an annual tax of $5, while black/white intermarriage was banned. This prohibition was subsequently extended in 1866 to anyone who was one-quarter or more Chinese or Hawaiian and one-half or more indigenous.[5] In this sense, Oregon was very much like California. Historian John Hittell, writing in the early 1860s, recorded California's similar exclusionary laws under the title of the "Inferiority of Colored Persons":

> All white male citizens are equal before the law of California; but negroes, Indians and Chinamen are not permitted to vote or to testify in the courts against white men. In a criminal case, one-eighth negro blood and one-half of Indian blood, in civil cases one-half of either, disqualifies a witness for testifying against a white man.[6]

By these provisions, if Governor James Douglas had been implicated in a Californian criminal proceeding, he certainly would have been precluded from giving evidence in a court of law. Indeed, his wife, Amelia, whose father was a Cree chief, would also have faced such discrimination.[7]

Much more could be said with regard to the policies of exclusion that largely originated in Oregon during the 1840s and whose consequences were felt decades later.[8] Such laws not only relegated ancient indigenous nations to less than a second-class citizenry; what is generally overlooked is that practically all HBC families, after an extended period of partnership with indigenous allies – a partnership that had built a shared, long-standing commerce – were now essentially pushed out to the British side of the new border. The romantic and economic relationships between fur traders and native women, known as the "custom of the country" had produced an ever-evolving but comparatively more inclusive fur-trade society, and it in many ways exemplified the colonial theories of Herman Merivale – to break with the past by partnering fully with, rather than persecuting, indigenous peoples.[9] This background of legislated racism south of the border is the often overlooked context in which to situate Fort Victoria and the Fraser River gold rush of 1858 as a home for persecuted peoples. When placed in this context,

Rules & Regulations, Issued in Conformity with the Gold Fields Act, 1859. To enforce order in the gold fields the colonial government printed small, portable copies of relevant laws, ideal for carrying in a pocket.
BCA NW 971.35 B862g

the British colonial offer of equality under the law for all becomes more than understandable and a unique welcome for the times.

While the fur trade north of the 49th parallel had fostered a unique relationship between British traders and indigenous allies and partners, the ethnic diversity is more complex. From a British perspective, there were the English but also the Celtic peoples – the Scottish, Irish, Cornish, Welsh and Manx among others. Also, there were the many different indigenous nations along the coast, such as the Lekwammen, Cowichan, Nuu-chah-nulth, or Kwakwa̱ka̱'wakw to name but a few (and in the interior, peoples such as the Nlaka'pamux, Secwepemc, St'at'imc and Tsilhquot'in). Inject into this mix the French Canadians and Métis, along with the Cree, Mohawk, Ojibwa and Iroquois, employed by the fur trade but originating from the central and prairie regions of British North America. Finally, there were significant numbers of Hawaiians employed in the fur trade and the Mexican people originally employed as muleteers for the HBC. Clearly, the fur trade was synonymous with ethnic diversity.

While American historian Susan Johnson concludes that the gold rushes were "among the most multiracial, multi-ethnic, multinational events that had yet occurred within the boundaries of the United States",[10] it must also be acknowledged that the lands known as Old Oregon (prior to the 1846 partition) had, in effect, already experienced a much longer period of such diversity. This multicultural world continued north of the border after 1846 and became immeasurably larger with the addition of gold seekers who, in many instances, were asylum seekers fleeing persecution. This is important context, as it provides one of the key reasons for the British Columbia gold rush experience unfolding much differently and in a comparatively more inclusive way.

The years that James Douglas held his governorships in the colonies of Vancouver Island and British Columbia (1851–64) are unique in terms of the gold rush manias that swept through California, Australia and other parts of the Pacific Rim. On July 8, 1858, Sir Edward Bulwer Lytton, secretary of state for the colonies, spoke in the British House of Commons with regard to this difference. Lytton introduced the Government of New Caledonia Bill and reflected on the changed circumstances brought by indigenous gold discoveries north of the border.[11] Lytton asserted that British Columbia, as the colony would later be called:

> is not like other colonies which have gone forth from these islands; and of which something is known of the character of the colonists.... As yet the rush of the adventurers is not for land but gold, not for a permanent settlement but for a speculative excursion. And, therefore, here *the immediate object is to establish temporary law and order* amidst a motley inundation of immigrant diggers, of whose antecedents we are wholly ignorant, and of whom perhaps few, if any, have any intention to become resident colonists and British subjects.[12]

Indeed, the protection of indigenous peoples was of paramount concern. "The most pressing and immediate care in this new colony," argued Lytton, "will be to preserve peace between the natives and the foreigners at the gold diggings."[13] Henry Labouchere, Lytton's predecessor, warned: "there was one circumstance which constituted the main danger of disorder, and that was the strong aversion which the Indians entertained towards the Americans."[14] The notorious genocidal actions levelled against the indigenous populations south of the border were well known to these British parliamentarians. The MP for Sheffield, John Arthur Roebuck, was more to the point, advancing the general anti-Californian view, such that "the whole ragamuffin population of the whole universe went there."[15] As a consequence, the establishment of British Columbia was unique in terms of other colonial possessions in that it had begun life with a population considered "quite as bad, if not worse" than California's.[16] "This colony was not like Australia or New Zealand," warned the Duke of Newcastle, "as remote from great Powers as from England – it was near to great Powers, but remote from us."[17] Viewed from afar, Britain's main concern was to ensure that the genocidal practices of California were not repeated in its colony.

While British Columbia is unique in having been charged by the Imperial government with protecting indigenous nations from the worst effects of the ever-expanding California mining frontier, this "New El Dorado"[18] also offered a safe haven for all those discriminated against in the Golden State, such as black Americans, Asians and Hispanics. For instance, writing in 1858 at the height of the Fraser River gold rush, Lord Napier, British Minister to the United States (1857–59), maintained:

> The Western movement ... now obeys a novel and powerful stimulus, the mineral fields of New Caledonia [British Columbia].... Every scheme for opening New Caledonia to the easy access of Emigrants

of British Birth and allegiance is worthy of the attention of Her Majesty's Government. Could the people of Canada and England be poured in equal numbers with those of the United States in the new Colony it would go far to neutralize many embarrassments and dangers, *nor will Her Majesty's Government undervalue the claims and services of the Indians, Negroes, Half-castes of all complexions or Asiatics, who, maltreated or excluded in the United States will again repair to a land, we trust of irreproachable equality and freedom with instincts of affection towards the British Crown.*[19]

The idea of a British Columbia "commonwealth" was, in effect, informed by the policies of British Liberal humanitarianism – as exemplified by William Wilberforce and the anti-slavery movement and, subsequently, through its offshoot, the Aborigines Protection Society, the 19th century's North American watchdog on indigenous rights. These influential groups kept a watchful eye on gold rush events along the Pacific Slope and were particularly mindful of the devastating actions of American miners south of the border. For instance: "From about 150,000 native people still living in California at the time of the [1848] gold discovery," states historian Jim Sandos, "that number had plummeted to 30,000 in 1860, an 80 per cent decline in just twelve years."[20] And Sandos attributes "the systematic murders of Indians by whites ... [as] the greatest single cause of death after 1848."[21]

Britain's policy was subsequently implemented by Governor James Douglas. Writing to the Duke of Newcastle, October 9, 1860, in the aftermath of the 1858 Fraser Canyon War[22], Douglas stated:

> I had the opportunity of communicating personally with the Native Indian Tribes, who assembled in great numbers at Cayoosh [Lillooet] during my stay. I made them clearly understand that Her Majesty's Government felt deeply interested in their welfare, and had sent instructions

that *they should be treated in all respects as Her Majesty's other subjects; and that the local Magistrates would tend to their complaints, and guard them from wrong* ... and that on their becoming registered Free Miners, they might dig and *search for Gold*, and hold mining claims on the same terms precisely as other miners; in short, *I strove to make them conscious that they were recognized members of the Commonwealth.*[23]

The Commonwealth Douglas spoke of was based on policies of inclusion (not surprising considering what had occurred to HBC families south of the border); it was a 'British California' that made sure to distinguish itself from the discriminatory practices found south of the 49th parallel.[24] At Rock Creek, BC, Douglas continued to emphasise the message of equality and freedom under the law for all, in contrast to the American gold fields. Douglas ensured that the Duke of Newcastle was informed fully in these matters.

> There was one subject which especially pre-occupied their minds ... namely the abject condition to which the cognate Native tribes of Oregon have been reduced by the American system of removing whole Tribes from their native homes into distant reserves where they are compelled to stay, and *denied the enjoyment of that natural freedom and liberty of action without which existence becomes intolerable.* They evidently looked forward with dread to their own future condition, fearing lest the same wretched fate awaited the native of British Columbia. I succeeded in disabusing their minds of those false impressions by fully explaining the view of Her Majesty's Government, and repeating in substance what ... was said on the same subject to the Assembled Tribes at Cayoosh [Lillooet] and Lytton. Those communications had the effect of re-assuring their minds and eliciting assurances of their fidelity and attachment.[25]

Douglas protected the rights of indigenous peoples – to the best of his abilities. Once again,

though with the exception of the Fraser Canyon War, it must be emphasised that British Columbia was different. In the post-1858 world, First Nations (women included), along with Chinese, are the main miners operating along the Fraser and Thompson rivers in subsequent years. Unlike their US counterparts, they were not targets of eradication through ongoing and violent conflict. In 1870 Thomas Basil Humphreys, member of the BC colonial legislature, highlighted the continued and valued importance of indigenous gold mining to British Columbia: "Take away the Indians from New Westminster, Lillooet, Lytton, Clinton," stated Humphreys, "and these towns would be nowhere.... At Lillooet I was told that there were upwards of 16,000; and $17,000 gold dust was purchased from Indians. Take away this trade and the towns must sink. I say, send them out to reservations and you destroy trade, and if the Indians are driven out we had all best go too."[26]

By 1858 the exclusionary policies and legislation inaugurated by the California state legislature increasingly disenfranchised and discriminated against the Afro-American people of California. Those affected held meetings in San Francisco, where it was decided to leave and relocate either to Sonora, Mexico or Vancouver Island for freedom's sake. A delegation was subsequently appointed to meet with Governor Douglas who welcomed these persecuted peoples and extended to them full rights of citizenship and equality under the law. Upon their return to San Francisco, the black delegation passed a further resolution that favoured relocating north. It reads in part:

> We are fully convinced that the continued aim of the spirit and policy of our mother country, is to oppress, degrade, and outrage us. We have, therefore, determined to seek asylum in the land of strangers, from oppression, prejudice and relentless persecution that have pursued us for more than two centuries in this our mother

country. Therefore, a delegation having been sent to Vancouver's Island, a place which had unfolded to us in our darkest hour, the prospect of a bright future; to this place of British possession, the delegation ... have fulfilled and rendered the most flattering accounts....[27]

With Douglas's guarantee, many black people from California moved north, including the civil rights activist Mifflin Wistar Gibbs[28], who had commenced his civil rights advocacy in the eastern US along with the famous abolitionist Frederick Douglass.[29] Gibbs left for California sometime in 1849–50 and recorded of his time in San Francisco that "they were ostracized, assaulted without redress, disenfranchised and denied their oath in a court of justice."[30] Gibbs viewed British Columbia as a land of freedom. Of their arrival in Victoria, Gibbs wrote:

Mifflin Wistar Gibbs, about 1873. BCA A-01601

> We received a warm welcome from the Governor [Douglas] and other officials of the colony, which was cheering. We had no complaint as to business patronage in the State of California, but there was ever present that spectre of oath denial and disenfranchisement; the disheartening consciousness that while our existence was tolerated, we were powerless to appeal to law for the protection of life or property when assailed. *British Columbia offered and gave protection to both, and equality of political privileges. I cannot describe with what joy we hailed the opportunity to enjoy that liberty under the "British Lion" denied us beneath the pinions of the American Eagle.* Three or four hundred coloured men from California and other States, with their families, settled in Victoria, drawn thither by the two-fold inducement – gold discovery and the assurance of enjoying impartiality the benefits of constitutional liberty. They built or bought homes and other property, and by industry and character vastly improved their condition *and were the recipients of respect and esteem from the community.*[31]

The reception received by the black Americans in 1858 was reminiscent of Gibbs' mentor, Frederick Douglass, who had visited Britain and Ireland in the previous decade. Arriving in Ireland in 1845, Douglass was struck by the seeming racial colour-blindness he encountered:

> I gaze around in vain for one who will question my equal humanity, claim me as his slave, or offer me an insult. I employ a cab – I am seated beside white people – I reach the hotel – I enter the same door – I am shown into the same parlour – I dine at the same table – and no one is offended.... I find myself regarded and treated at every turn with kindness

and deference paid to white people. When I go to church, I am met by no upturned nose and scornful lip to tell me, "We don't allow niggers in here!"[32]

This positive reception is seemingly comparable to that given Gibbs and other black Americans in Victoria. While in Britain in 1846, Douglass met Thomas Clarkson, one of the last living British abolitionists, who had persuaded Parliament to abolish slavery in Great Britain and its colonies. Undoubtedly, Douglass' experience in Britain would have been well-known to Gibbs and a further incentive to relocate to the New El Dorado of the north.

While it must be acknowledged that there was racial prejudice in Victoria through the early gold rush period, much of this anti-black sentiment left with Americans returning to the US at the outset of the American Civil War. Evidence is that Gibbs was subsequently elected in 1866 to Victoria city council representing James Bay. He was the first black councillor in the city and served for a time as the acting mayor. He also was a delegate to the Yale Convention organized by Amor De Cosmos for discussions related to BC's entry into the Canadian Confederation.[33] Gibbs returned to the United States in 1869, and with the assistance of his early legal training in Victoria, became the first black American judge in that country.

Like their black counterparts, the Chinese of California were increasingly discriminated against by exclusionary legislation and also through a systemic racism levelled towards Asian peoples who were routinely driven from their rich placer claims in the Sierra Nevada Range. As Hittell wrote of California's "Anti-Chinese Mob" in the early 1860s:

> The white miners have a great dislike to Chinamen, who are frequently driven away from their claims, and expelled from districts by mobs. In such cases the officers of the law do not ordinarily interfere, and no matter how much the unfortunate yellow men may be beaten or despoiled, the law does not attempt to restore them to their rights or avenge their wrongs.[34]

By 1855 a petition attributed to Chinese merchants based in San Francisco made an appeal to the American public asking that their rights be respected:

> TO THE AMERICAN CITIZENS. – Americans: We, the undersigned, Chinese merchants, come before you to plead our cause, and that of our countrymen, residents of San Francisco, or diffused throughout California.
>
> We come to ask for the moral and industrious of our race liberty to remain in this State, and to continue peaceably and without molestation in our various labours and pursuits.... Neither injustice or severity has been spared us.... *Instead of the equality and protection which seemed to be promised by the laws of a great nation to those who seek a shelter under its flag, an asylum upon its territory, we find only inequality and oppression.*
>
> Frequently before the Courts of Justice, where our evidence is not even listened to – where, if it obtain a hearing, by favour, but rarely is any account made of it. Inequality before public opinion – which is so far, apparently, from considering us as men, that many of your countrymen feel no scruple in making our lives their sport, and in using us as the object of their cruel amusement. Oppression by the Law, which subjects us to exorbitant taxes imposed upon us exclusively – oppression without the pale of the law, which refuses us its protection, and leaves us a prey to vexations and humilities, which it seems to invoke upon our heads by placing us in an exceptional position.
>
> Believe us, we have exaggerated nothing in this picture.... We see well that you appear to desire our departure ... [but] can they, at a given moment, provide themselves with the means of *quitting this country in a body, in order to seek elsewhere some less inhospitable land?*[35]

It has been stated that the 1855 session of the California legislature "was perhaps the high-water mark of anti-Chinese sentiment" for the whole of

Chinese prospector crossing the Ashcroft Bridge, about 1882. BCA C-01274

the 1850s.[36] It is likely that just as "Captain Jeremiah Nagle of the SS *Commodore* had discussed the plight of the blacks in California with James Douglas during the early spring of 1858 when discrimination there was at a peak" (resulting in Douglas's invitation to blacks "to settle under the freedom of the British flag"), a similar, inclusive stance would have been extended to the persecuted Chinese of California.[37]

Two of the many Chinese businesses that were apparent signatories to this 1855 petition were those of Sam Wo and Hop Kee, and just three years later, in 1858, Hop Kee & Company had contracted Governor Douglas's favoured merchant house in San Francisco (Allan, Lowe & Company) to transport 300 Chinese people to Victoria.[38] It was further recorded in the California press that these companies were part of the original scramble for Victoria town lots. The *Sacramento Daily Union* reported: "Sam Wo & Co., and Hop Kee & Co., the Chinese merchants, have purchased an entire square for Chinese purposes. No more lots are now sold by the Government; the rush on the land office was so great that it was thought proper to close it."[39] The San Francisco *Bulletin* reported that three of the leading "aristocratic" Chinese businessmen had left on the *Panama* for the Fraser River Mines to prospect the country and make further preparations for those who would follow. The newspaper further suggested "that nearly the entire Chinese population ... will leave for the British Possessions."[40]

While the indigenous peoples of California were unable to escape the abuses committed in their birthplace, many black and Chinese travelled north for freedom. In the period before Confederation with Canada (1858–1871), Chinese miners – like all other gold seekers regardless of ethnicity – were not forced to pay a foreign "head tax"[41] but rather participated in a universally applied Crown licensing system.

In Victoria a transnational merchant class, composed of blacks, Chinese, Jews, Americans, Canadians and Europeans, conducted their business with the full and equal protection of the law. In fact, Chinese leaders were members of the local Chamber of Commerce and in 1864, upon the retirement of James Douglas, presented a memorial to the new governor that emphasized their appreciation of the freedom gained since departing California. The address, as reported in the *British Colonist* stated:

Us Chinese men greeting Thee Excellency in first degree Arthur Edward Kennedy.... All us here be dwellers at Victoria, this Island, and British Columbia, much wish to shew mind of dutiful loyalty to this Kingdom Mother Queen Victoria, for much square and equal Kingdom rule of us....

This Kingdom rule very different from China. Chinese mind feel much devoted to Victoria Queen, *for the protection and distributive rule of him Excellency old Governor Sir James Douglas, so reverse California ruling when applied to us Chinese country men....* In ending, us confident in gracious hope in thee, first degree and first rank, and first link, *and trust our Californian neighbours may not exercise prejudice to our grief.* [42]

Upon receiving the address, Governor Kennedy, with the assistance of a translator, replied to prominent Victorian Lee Chang and the Chinese delegation guaranteeing that the policy of the Douglas years would continue:

A stock certificate issued by Selim Franklin, the first Jew elected to a British North American legislature, to Lee Chang, a prominent business leader in Victoria's Chinatown. BCA MS-1053 (Knowlton Collection)

It was the desire of her Gracious Majesty the Queen and the Imperial Government to render equal justice to people of every nationality in her dominions, and he assured them that the Chinese population in this colony would be protected in their lives and property as well as any other of her subjects. His Excellency said he thought very highly of the sentiments expressed in their address, and said they showed a great knowledge of trade and commercial principles. He hoped they would also show the community that they would not be wanting in obedience to the laws, *and they might depend on always receiving the protection of the laws.*[43]

James Douglas's final word with regard to the black people of California applies to other ethnic minorities that also fled north to escape persecution. "I am glad that Her Majesty's Government ... generously grants, within the Colony of Vancouver's Island, *a refuge for political exiles*, provided they yield obedience to the Laws, and avoid public scandals, and lead quiet and honest lives."[44] Certainly the attraction of British Columbia was gold, but for those outside full American citizenship, the British colonies represented much more than the potential for economic gain. The New El Dorado also represented gains in political and social well-being.

Indeed, Governor Douglas, the mixed-blood "Father of British Columbia," had countered the discriminatory policies of California in keeping with the spirit of Liberal humanitarianism, the longstanding HBC-indigenous partnership and his own first-hand observation of racial persecution south of the border. As historian Kevin Starr succinctly stated: "White Americans miserably failed to respond positively to the possibilities of the multiracial, multi-ethnic society that had materialized itself in California."[45] But British Columbia, prior to joining the Canadian Confederation in 1871, ultimately confronted the worst aspects of these gold rushes that threw so many peoples together and produced a substantially greater civil society with freedom under the law for all. Unfortunately, this welcoming period of equality did not last long beyond Douglas's time as governor – in fact it was overturned by later exclusionary laws and overtly sanctioned discriminatory practises – but it is a moment in time that needs to be reasserted and is a past that must be remembered. ✗

ACKNOWLEDGEMENTS

I would like to thank the Royal BC Museum for inviting me to their consultation meetings to discuss with members of the black, Chinese and Jewish organizations the views found within this essay with respect to the British Columbia Commonwealth.

NOTES

1   James Douglas held office under the provisional government as a local district judge for three years.

2   John C. Jackson, *Children of the Fur Trade: Forgotten Métis of the Pacific Northwest* (Missoula, Montana: Mountain Press, 1995), p. 218.

3   Ibid., p. 223.

4   Ibid., p. 222.

5   Stacey L. Smith, "Oregon's Civil War: The Troubled Legacy of Emancipation in the Pacific Northwest," *Oregon Historical Quarterly*, 115:2 (Summer 2014), p. 169. See also K. Keith Richard, "Unwelcome Settlers: Black and Mulatto Oregon Pioneers," *Oregon Historical Quarterly*, 84:1 (Spring, 1983), p. 45.

6   John S. Hittell, *The Resources of California: Comprising Agriculture, Mining, Geography, Climate, Commerce, &c. 2nd edition* (San Francisco: A. Roman and Company, 1866), p. 350. For an example of a typical Californian gold rush narrative of the period that contains several anti-Chinese passages, see the classic work by Frank Marryat, *Mountains and Molehills; Or Recollections of a Burnt Journal* (London: Longman, Brown, Green, and Longmans, 1855, reprint, Philadelphia and New York: J.B. Lippincott Company, 1962), pp. 172–76.

7   Douglas was the son of a Scottish sugar planter and a free coloured West Indian. John Adams, *Old Square-Toes and His Lady: The Life of James and Amelia Douglas* (Victoria, BC: Horsdal & Schubart, 2001), pp. 1–3.

8   The infamous "Lash Law" of 1844, though lasting less than a year, directed that blacks, whether slave or free, be whipped twice a year "until he or she shall quit the territory." See R. Gregory Nokes, *Breaking Chains: Slavery on Trial in the Oregon Territory* (Corvallis: Oregon State University Press, 2013), p. 47.

9   Herman Merivale lectured at Oxford and subsequently was appointed to the Colonial Office, becoming the permanent under-secretary of state for the colonies. See Merivale, *Lectures on Colonization and Colonies Delivered before the University of Oxford in 1839, 1840 and 1841* (London: 1841).

10 Susan Lee Johnson, *Roaring Camp: The Social World of the California Gold Rush* (New York & London: W.W. Norton, 2000), p. 12.

11 Daniel Marshall, "Rickard Revisited: Native 'Participation' in the Gold Discoveries of British Columbia," *Native Studies Review* 11:1 (1997), pp. 91–108.

12 Speech of Sir Edward Bulwer Lytton, "Government of New Caledonia Bill," 2nd Reading, July 8, 1858 in *Hansard's Parliamentary Debates: Third Series*. CLI (London: Cornelius Buck, 1858), pp. 1100–1102. Emphasis added.

13 Lytton, House of Commons, July 8, 1858. *Hansard's Parliamentary Debates: Third Series*. CLI, p. 1104.

14 Labouchere, July 8, 1858. Ibid., pp. 1107–08. Roderick Finlayson, in charge of Fort Victoria before Douglas' arrival, stated that HBC personnel always passed through indigenous territories safely, while "Boston Men", or Americans, were shot on sight. Roderick Finlayson Reminiscences, British Columbia Manuscript Collection, Bancroft Library, University of California, Berkeley.

15 Roebuck, July 19, 1858. Ibid., p. 1766.

16 Ibid., p. 1767.

17 Newcastle, House of Lords, July 26, 1858. Ibid., p. 2103.

18 British Columbia became increasingly known as "The New El Dorado." For instance, see Kinahan Cornwallis, *The New El Dorado; Or, British Columbia* (London: Thomas Cautley Newby, 1858).

19 Lord Napier, British minister to Washington, DC, to Lord Malmesbury, foreign secretary, July 30, 1858, in London Correspondence between the HBC and HM Government, 1858–59, Hudson's Bay Company Archives, Winnipeg. Emphasis added.

20 James A. Sandos, "'Because he is a liar and a thief': Conquering the Residents of 'Old' California, 1850–1880," chapter 4 as found in *Rooted in Barbarous Soil: People, Culture, and Community in Gold Rush California*, Kevin Starr and Richard J. Orsi, eds (Berkeley & London: University of California Press, 2000), p. 96.

21 Ibid.

22 See the made-for-TV documentary *Canyon War: The Untold Story* (Wunderman Films, 2009).

23 Douglas to Newcastle, October 9, 1860, No. 11678, CO 60/8. Emphasis added.

24 Let me clarify what I mean by the term *commonwealth*. I use this term in the sense of "public welfare; general good or advantage," and this meaning dates from the 15th century. The original phrase "the common-wealth" or "the common weal" comes from the old meaning of "wealth," which is "well-being." The term literally means "common well-being." In the 17th century the definition of "commonwealth" expanded from its original sense of "public welfare" or "commonweal" to mean "a state in which the supreme power is vested in the people."

25 Douglas to Newcastle, October 9, 1860, No. 11678, CO 60/8. Emphasis added.

26 Thomas Basil Humphreys, March 25, 1870, Confederation Debate, *Journals of the Colonial Legislatures*, James E. Hendrickson, ed., V, pp. 567–68.

27 "Another Meeting of the Colored People," San Francisco *Bulletin*, May 21, 1858, p. 3. Emphasis added.

28 Gibbs was a member of the Underground Railroad and the Philadelphia Antislavery Society. He was subsequently "persuaded by Frederick Douglass and Charles Lenox Redmond to begin a career as an antislavery lecturer." See William Loren Katz, *The Black West*, 3rd ed. (Seattle: Open Hand Publishing, 1987), pp. 139–42, and also "The Black Pioneers of British Columbia," pp. 81–81.

29 Frederick Douglass (1881–1895) was a black American social reformer, speaker, writer and statesman who, after escaping from slavery, became a leader of the American abolitionist movement. He was known for his remarkable speeches and anti-slavery writing. He provided a good example against slaveholders' arguments that slaves did not possess the intellectual capacity to function as independent citizens.

30 Taken from Mifflin Wistar Gibbs, *Shadow and Light: An Autobiography* (1902), p. 46.

31 Ibid., p. 63. Emphasis added. It is not surprising that Gibbs and other expatriate black Americans followed Governor

James Douglas, Dr Helmcken and others to Bishop Cridge's Episcopalian church at the head of James Bay after the break with Christ Church up the hill. Cridge welcomed them with open arms. See Ian Macdonald and Betty O'Keefe, *Quiet Reformers: The Legacy of Early Victoria's Bishop Edward and Mary Cridge* (Vancouver: Ronsdale Press, 2010).

32 Frederick Douglass, *My Bondage and My Freedom* (1855), p. 371.

33 Gibbs' daughter, Ida Alexander Gibbs Hunt, born in Victoria in 1862 (corner of Michigan and Menzies streets), also became a highly educated civil rights leader of note, having attended the Second Pan-African Congress in Paris in 1919 as the organization's assistant secretary. Ida Gibbs Hunt was also one of the very first black women to receive a Bachelor's degree in the United States after the Civil War.

34 Hittell, *The Resources of California*, p. 375.

35 "The Appeal of the Chinese Merchants," September 12, 1855, *Sacramento Daily Union*. Emphasis added.

36 Charles J. McClain, "The Chinese Struggle for Civil Rights in Nineteenth Century America: The First Phase, 1850– 1870," *California Law Review* 72:532 (1984), p. 545.

37 Adams, *Old Square-Toes and His Lady*, p. 121.

38 Business records of Kwong Lee and Co., and Hop Kee and Co., including shares of British Columbia companies and agreement to transport Chinese to Victoria. Knowlton Collection, Original, 1858–1887, MS-1053, BC Archives. For an 1858 account of the HBC overruling Californians in their attempt to prevent the entry of these early Chinese gold seekers from landing at Fort Hope, BC, see Daniel Marshall, "Mapping the New El Dorado: The Fraser River Gold Rush and the Appropriation of Native Space," *Interpreting Canada's Past: A Pre-Confederation Reader*, 4th ed., J.M. Bumstead, Len Kuffert and Michel Ducharme, eds (Oxford University Press, 2011), pp. 409–11.

39 "Frazer River Diggings," June 24, 1858, *Sacramento Daily Union*. The original, leather-bound Victoria town lot register for 1858 is still held by the Surveyor-General's Office and records the Chinese property purchases that established Canada's oldest Chinatown.

40 "The Yellow Fever in San Francisco," *Bulletin*, May 21, 1858, p. 2. Also, "Chinese Agencies at the Fraser River Mines," *Bulletin*, May 24, 1858, p. 2.

41 Like both the black and Chinese peoples of California, the story of discrimination levelled against Mexicans, Chileans or other gold seekers from Central and South America is obviously similar. The institution of a foreign miners head tax had caused, as historian Rodman Paul noted, "many Latin Americans to quit California forever." Rodman W. Paul, *California Gold: The Beginning of the Mining in the Far West* (Lincoln: University of Nebraska Press, 1947), p. 111.

42 "Chinese Address to the Governor," *British Colonist*, April 5, 1864, p. 3. Signed Tai Soong & Co., by Tong Kee; Yan, Woo Sang & Co., by Chang Tsoo; Kwong Lee & Co., by Lee Chang, Tong Fat. Emphasis added.

43 Ibid.

44 Douglas to Labouchere, secretary of state for the colonies, April 6, 1858, No. 14, CO 305/9. Emphasis added.

45 Kevin Starr, "Rooted in Barbarous Soil: An Introduction to Gold Rush Society and Culture," in *Rooted in Barbarous Soil: People, Culture, and Community in Gold Rush California*, Kevin Starr and Richard J. Orsi, eds (Berkeley: University of California Press, 2000), p. 6.

Images and Intention

Early British Columbian Gold Rushes Seen Through the Works of Painters and Photographers

Don Bourdon

|||||||||||||||||||||||||||||||||||||||||||||||

A SOLITARY PROSPECTOR swirls a pan full of gravel and ice-cold water, gradually reducing the volume, hoping against hope that gold will lie at the bottom. His few worldly possessions lay around him. The eye is drawn up-stream, suggesting almost endless creeks and valleys that might hold golden riches.

Wonderful landscape and human interest images from early British Columbia gold rushes, such as William G.R. Hind's *Prospecting For Alluvial Gold in British Columbia*, have survived in the forms of sketches, paintings and photographs. One hundred and fifty years later, we wonder how well these works capture the essence of life and landscape in the goldfields. The artists' and photographers' choices of their subjects and how to depict them influences our understanding. But, in spite of the creators' biases, the body of work gives modern viewers insight into specific places and phenomena as well as a glimpse into the psyche of the gold seeker.

British artists and photographers followed the lure of gold and promise of adventure. They brought their topographical skills, their familiarity with the picturesque, beautiful, and sublime and an understanding of their audiences. Some followed "the long-established impulse to observe and record precisely what nature present[ed] to the eye … for empiricism was an integral part of the British temperament."[1] Others succeeded in conveying emotion that spans the intervening years and brings some insight into avarice, exploitation, destruction and a disregard for the original inhabitants of the land – all in the slim hope of striking it rich.

Prospecting for Alluvial Gold in British Columbia, 1864.
William G.R. Hind, oil on card. BCA PDP02612

Art historian Berenice Gilmore, in her ground-breaking study *Artists Overland*, argues that British Columbia had a profound effect on artists who depicted its places and people before the completion of the transcontinental railway in 1885:

> Practically no attempt was made to make paintings of a formal kind; the amateur artists painted what they saw, tempered only by appreciation of the land; the professional artists tended to be caught off guard by the magnificence of what they saw, and discarding rules, painted the country in the bright colours that represented not only the scene before them, but the intangible feelings conveyed by this new and beautiful place, inhabited by people different from those they were used to, in surroundings strange and wonderful.[2]

Gilmore's observation applies to artists who followed BCs early gold rushes of the late 1850s and 1860s in places as "strange and wonderful" as could be imagined: vast stretches of untouched mountain ranges; powerful rivers coursing through deep canyons; waterlogged placer mining towns amid hills denuded of trees; hard-bitten gold miners, freighters and settlers at lonely road houses or toiling on frigid gold creeks. The artists and photographers active during the Fraser and Cariboo gold rushes captured "what they saw" driven by a desire to share faithful images of the West with far-off audiences. Those audiences, full of romantic ideas about the quest for gold, were thirsting for imagery. Painting and photography competed for supremacy; the first could convey action, colour and drama, while the second claimed to be the messenger of truth in spite of the selective eye of the photographer. Authenticity of these representations served practical ends, as artists and photographers were creating source material for published engravings. However, some of these images transcend empiricism. As the beneficiaries of these paintings, drawings and photographs we enjoy their authenticity and try to understand the emotional response that brought them into being.

Jasper's House, about 1864.
William G.R. Hind, watercolour on paper. BCA PDP00407

Four gold rush painters and two photographers whose work is held in the BC Archives collections created images that convey the excitement, challenges and beauty of the era. Their works were reproduced in the new illustrated press and in books, as well as in anticipation of creating larger works for exhibition and sale. New printing technology, publishing economies and photographic capabilities extended the reach of this imagery. Though some were never intended for reproduction, publishers frequently used paintings and uncredited photographs without permission. Whether amateur or professional, painter or photographer, all shared a desire to portray the new land and people's place within it.

BC gold-rush images show newcomers exploring, exploiting and settling in often harsh but awe-inspiring landscapes. Some images, particularly photographs, make a point of featuring First Peoples, little known or understood by outsiders. Or, they were simply made to show people "back home" the sense of place and peoples' relationships with it.

The sketches and paintings are quite small and portable, precursors of larger works or grist for the publishing mill. Watercolour was the prevailing choice of painters, compact and well-suited to travel and embraced as the ideal medium for the topographic landscape. The photographic views, too, are generally limited in size to a maximum of 8 x 10 inches (20.4 x 25.5 cm), the typical glass-negative format. These were made by professional photographers for purchase by travellers and residents as photography was beyond the grasp of all but a very few. In spite of their small sizes, the images are arresting. One hundred fifty years later, they delight, inform and challenge us, just as they did armchair explorers of the 19th century.

WILLIAM HIND: OVERLANDER

IN 1927, British Columbia's gold rushes of the 1860s were within living memory for only a few former participants. Provincial Archivist John Hosie (1881–1934) was keenly aware that documentation of the Fraser and Cariboo rushes needed his attention if records and recollections were to be preserved. That year, he tracked down a trove of paintings by English/Canadian artist William George Richardson Hind (1833–89). Journalist Bruce Hutchison wrote of the archivist's discovery:

> A chance clue set Mr Hosie on the trail of these paintings and sketches, which he finally ran to earth lying forgotten and little prized in a portfolio in the artist's old home in New Brunswick. They

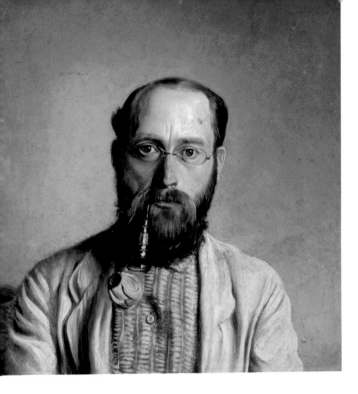

have not suffered by the passing of time, however, being today just as fresh and bright as when the artist completed them. There are fifteen in the set, and happily one of them is a picture of Mr Hind himself about the size of a modern cabinet photograph.[3]

This collection formed only a fraction of a vast series of sketches and paintings by William G.R. Hind. In 1944 the archives augmented this group with seven more Hind works purchased for $22. Because Hind's output was vast and covered a huge geographic span from Labrador to British Columbia, the artist's works reside in a number of institutions and private collections.[4]

Renowned professor and curator Dennis Reid maintains that Hind belongs to the history of Canadian art, not British. Hind's formidable creativity transcends the topographical approach of immigrant artists. His western paintings depict hirsute prospectors panning for gold and wading through Cariboo streams; miners at work and leisure; and an "Overlander" heading west on foot, leading a pack ox over the Rockies high above Jasper House. Man and beast trudge slowly toward the Cariboo across the very crown of the continent (see *Jasper's House*). Hind's landscapes and human-interest studies are executed in painstaking detail and startling colours consistent with the Pre-Raphaelites. His compositions are truly unorthodox, some as compressed and confined as others are expansive.

Hind's work was forgotten until an exhibition was mounted in 1967 by Russell Harper. Art historians struggled to fit Hind into a niche. He was derided as "primitive" and doubtless influenced by the Pre-Raphaelites. Little was known of his life beyond what could be ascertained from his artworks and a smattering of documents and newspaper accounts. Then Ottawa art curator Gilbert L. Gignac discovered records attesting to the practical nature of Hind's art education and one of his primary motives. Hind and his brother Henry Youle Hind (1823–1908) envisioned publications on the emerging Dominion of Canada that would be illustrated with colour engravings and lithographs. Gignac's discoveries were incorporated into an exhibition and catalogue curated by Mary Jo Hughes in 2002: *Hindsight: William Hind in the Canadian West.*[5]

Hind was born and educated in Nottingham, England. He studied at the Government School of Art and Design there, one of a number of government schools "developed to teach artists the discipline of drawing and painting as a practical and functional tool in industry and society". This was a vastly different approach from traditional Royal Academy training. Hind was trained as a teacher and illustrator. In 1851, at the age of 18, he arrived in Canada and began working as the teacher of drawing at Normal and Model Schools in Toronto, where he taught until 1857.

Hind's older brother, Henry Youle Hind was an explorer, professor and self-styled geologist. His extensive explorations resulted in reports

British Columbia Miners, 1864. William G.R. Hind, watercolour on card. BCA PDP00014

that required illustrative material. In 1857 he accompanied the Canadian Red River Exploring Expedition as a geologist and in 1858 returned to the plains as director in charge of the Assiniboine and Saskatchewan Exploring Expedition. Back home, he enlisted his younger brother's talents in creating illustrations, because he was dissatisfied with the sketches and photographs made by other expedition members. William's role expanded from copyist to expedition artist on an 1861 journey up the Moisie River in Labrador. Henry Hind led the expedition and published *Explorations in the Interior of the Labrador Peninsula: The Country of the Montagnais and Nasquapee Indians* in 1863. William illustrated the report with 90 paintings of landscapes and First Peoples of Labrador. Some became engravings.

Based on his earlier explorations, Henry Hind published a booklet in 1862: *A Sketch of an Over-land Route to British Columbia*. This booklet presaged his dream of major publications on Canada. It helped inflame William's desire to see and paint the West and that year, he joined a party of gold seekers in Toronto intent on reaching the Cariboo by land. The group travelled with Red River carts but mainly on foot. William Hind made hundreds of sketches on the epic trek to the gold fields.

Hind's sketches and paintings demonstrate a keen eye for detail, some executed with a high degree of realism. His prospectors and miners cut romantic figures, but his eye for accuracy ensured that details were recorded: hole-ridden hats, characteristic shirts, knives and pipes and in an age of profuse facial hair even larger than fashionable beards. Prospecting and placer gold mining equipment is carefully executed. On closer examination, though, a question surfaces: was Hind

Miners, BC, about 1864. William G.R. Hind, oil on board. BCA PDP00032

Miner, Rocky Mountains, 1864. William G.R. Hind, watercolour on card. BCA PDP00028

fascinated by an idealized miner-type? In six extant self-portraits, Hind begins to resemble characters he immortalized.

Hind's prototypical prospector-miner is substantiated by eye-witness accounts. In 1916, artist Eleanor Fellows, writing as Eleanor C. Smyth, described "up-country" veterans of the 1860s:

> Here in Victoria they landed in crowds, quietly, gravely, hardly vouchsafing a glance at anybody or anything, and went their way without fuss or hesitation…. Sombrero on head, bowie-knife in small back trouser pocket, revolvers in broad sash or ample waist-belt, the loose blouse we used to call a "garibaldi" clothing the upper person, the long "gum" boots reaching to the knees which enabled their wearer to work with impunity in water for hours together, the tightly-rolled blanket and gold-mining implements upon the back and shoulders, each man looked thoroughly "fit" and ready for the strenuous life before him.[6]

Fellows' description aptly fits Hind's miners. Perhaps, though, the artist is playing a trick in *Miners in the Leather Pass, Rocky Mountains, 1864*. As Reid has pointed out, these miners are so similar they could be one and the same man: the self-same in ascent and having reached his goal, taking a pipe during a rest.

Like most of the overlanders exhausted by their journey, Hind stayed briefly in the gold fields before continuing to Victoria, where he established a studio. He returned to the interior in 1864. Several of his paintings in the BC Archives bear that date. Hind eked out a living in Victoria as a painter of pictures and signs. He left for Winnipeg in 1870 and went on to the Maritimes, where he lived for the remainder of his life. In tribute Reid states: "he was one of those private, intensely personal artists that Canada has been blessed with from time to time – a man *of* his time."[7]

Miners in the Leather Pass, Rocky Mountains, 1864. William G.R. Hind, watercolour on paper. BCA PDP01214

EDWARD M. RICHARDSON
ARTIST OF RICHFIELD

THOUGH HIND IS THE PRE-EMINENT ARTIST of British Columbia's early gold rushes, others contributed to the body of works in the BC Archives collections. Edward M. Richardson (?–1874), like Hind, filled his watercolours with human interest. Richardson was the son of a sculptor and a student of Sir George Hayter at the Royal Academy School in England. He arrived in Victoria around 1862 and painted in Cariboo camps in 1863, painting men battling physical obstacles in search of placer gold. He too painted the red-shirted prospector.

Surviving works suggest he produced multiples of the same scenes for sale to those in the goldfields or back in Victoria. He strategically placed a figure in two nearly identical views of the mining town of Richfield on Williams Creek[8] and also inserted a tiny string of pack animals. Placing people within

landscape paintings was, of course, a common way to provide a sense of scale as well as assert man's role in transforming nature. Apparently, Richardson, the topographer and student of human nature, raffled off his paintings in Victoria's St Nicholas Billiard Hall in 1865.[9]

Untitled, about 1863. Edward M. Richardson, watercolour on paper. BCA PDP00104

Richfield, Williams Creek, about 1863. Edward M. Richardson, watercolour on paper. BCA PDP00103

CHARLES GENTILE
GENTLEMAN PHOTOGRAPHER

THE ACCURACY of Richardson's Richfield views is supported by Charles Gentile's photographs. Charles (or Carlo) Gentile (1835–93) was an Italian gentleman-adventurer and intrepid wet-plate practitioner who created important photographs of First Peoples and landscapes in Canada and the United States. He conducted photography under trying field conditions using the fussy and cumbersome wet-plate collodion process. In spite of the difficulties of carrying glass plates and chemicals and the necessity of sensitizing and fixing plates on the spot the process was a technological breakthrough at the time. It allowed photographers to generate multiple prints from glass-plate nega-

tives. Gentile operated a portrait studio in Victoria from 1862 to 1866 and photographed extensively throughout the interior of the colony in 1865, including Williams Creek. His view of Richfield in 1865 confirms the fidelity of Richardson's landscapes painted about two years earlier. The scenes are very similar though further deforestation is apparent in Gentile's later image.

The absence of people in Gentile's landscapes seems strange, until one considers the long exposure times necessary to obtain a photograph. Stopping action was impossible. Unless people stood motionless for the seconds-long exposures, they simply passed out of the photograph or registered

Richfield, 1865. Charles Gentile, albumen print. BCA G-00795

Bedrock flume, Williams Creek, 1865. Charles Gentile, albumen print. BCA G-00797

as a blur. *Bedrock flume, Williams Creek* includes one of the few women visible on the creeks in 1865. The woman and her male companions are dressed in fine clothes juxtaposed against a harsh landscape ravaged by mining activity. Gentile's photographs served as a basis for a number of engravings.[10]

FREDERICK WHYMPER
ARTIST, ADVENTURER AND WRITER

PROFESSIONAL ARTIST, ENGRAVER, adventurer and writer Frederick Whymper (1838–1901) came from an accomplished family of artists and engravers. His parents were English watercolourists

Upper Entrance to the Defile, Bute Inlet, 1864. Frederick Whymper, watercolour on paper. BCA PDP00105

Left: *The Frazer, From Nicaragua Slide (near the Zigzag), 1863*. Frederick Whymper, watercolour on paper. The Zigzag was a treacherous set of switchbacks on a trail high above the canyon floor. BCA PDP00107

and his younger brother was a star mountaineer of the 1860s, conqueror of the Matterhorn, and later a celebrity in the Canadian Rockies. Frederick Whymper came to Victoria in 1862 at the height of the gold rush excitement and established a studio. The next year, he embarked on "a sketching and pedestrian tour" to the goldfields.

Whymper travelled extensively in search of art subjects and adventure stories for publication. He ventured to the Cariboo where he made paintings, accompanied Alfred Waddington's road construction party to Bute Inlet just prior to the Chilcotin Uprising, and participated in the Vancouver Island Exploratory and the Collins Overland Telegraph expeditions. Explorations in Yukon and Alaska gave rise to the book, *Travels and Adventure in* the Territory of Alaska (1869), which includes six engravings of scenes in British Columbia. Whymper is credited with being the first traveller to report the presence of gold in the Yukon.

Like Richardson, the mark of man's enterprise on the landscape is a central feature of Whymper's work. *Williams Creek from the Canyon to Middle Town (Barkerville)* is a faithful illustration of the inevitable destruction of a valley bottom in the interests of mining. Miners operating windlasses and waterwheels enliven this work.

Engravings from Whymper's watercolours appeared in *Harpers Magazine, Illustrated Travels* and scientific journals.[11] Multiple views of subjects such as the village of Yale on the Fraser suggest that the artist was making a living selling his paintings. After several years in British Columbia, Whymper worked in San Francisco as a journalist. He returned to England in the late 1870s or early '80s. His watercolours are vivid reminders of life in the gold fields.

Williams Creek from the Canyon to Middle Town (Barkerville), 1863. Frederick Whymper, sepia on paper. BCA PDP00111

William's Creek from the Cañon to Middle Town (Barkerville)

Yates Street – No. 4, 1860. Sarah Crease, watercolour on paper. BCA PDP02894

SARAH CREASE
"A COLONIAL AMATEUR"

THERE IS NO DOUBT as to the veracity of Sarah Crease's paintings. She was an immigrant artist who stayed and became fully engaged in Victorian society. Sarah Crease (1823–1922) was born in London to botanist John Lindley and Sarah Freestone. She thrived in an environment of scientific enquiry and artistic excellence and became an accomplished amateur artist after learning wood-block printing and engraving techniques. She and her young family followed her husband, barrister Henry Pering Pellew Crease, to Vancouver Island in 1860.

That year, she made a series of 12 lively and realistic watercolour paintings of Fort Victoria and the town that was rapidly surrounding it to send home to her parents so that they could picture her new home so far away. This series was exhibited before a large audience at the 1862 International Exhibition in London, credited as "the work of a colonial amateur".[12] Several of these paintings were reproduced in Richard C. Mayne's *Four years in British Columbia and Vancouver Island* (1862), unfortunately misattributed to "Dr Lindley"; they

A Street in Victoria, Vancouver Island.
Richard C. Mayne, tinted engraving,
after Sarah Crease.[14] BCA PDP01892

also appeared as lithographic illustrations in other publications over the years.[13]

Though Sarah Crease did not travel to the gold fields in the 1860s, she made sketches in New Westminster, Yale and several of the gravel bars along the Fraser River. Her Victoria scenes are especially important as early works documenting the colonial centre fuelled by gold rush wealth. Their sense of motion and bustle makes them particularly endearing. Much of their vitality and accuracy is lost in the engravings created after they were sent home to England.

FREDERICK DALLY
PROLIFIC PHOTOGRAPHER
OF BRITISH COLUMBIA

FREDERICK DALLY'S PHOTOGRAPHS have come to represent the gold rush era in our collective consciousness. Like folk songs, they are familiar, but their origin unknown. Frederick Dally (1838–1914) was a prolific wet-plate portrait and landscape photographer who practiced in Victoria between 1866 and 1870 and had a studio in Barkerville for two years. His stock in trade was portraiture catering to the *carte de visite* rage.[15] Many Cariboo adventurers had their likenesses – made in San Francisco, Victoria or even Barkerville – sent home to prove that they were thriving.

Dally's landscapes and commissioned photographs of mining operations have strong human interest. Like the painters preceding him, the inclusion of the human figure provides a

Shaft entrance to Sheepshead Claim, Williams Creek, about 1868. Frederick Dally, albumen print. BCA A-02049

sense of scale and proof of industry. His Cariboo photographs date from 1867. By that time mining had evolved beyond the days of Hind's and Richardson's colourful prototypical prospectors. Mining companies had formed, were capitalized and employed wage labour. These labourers and mine owners are depicted in Dally's mining photographs. That said, his on-site portrait titled *Bill Phinney with Hand Rocker* is as evocative

as Hind's hardy prospector, though their circumstances, separated by only five years, are so different. Dally's iconic images of the Cariboo Wagon Road document an engineering wonder and the freight wagons and teams travelling over it. Once again, man has overcome nature's impediments.

Dally made a specialty of photographing First Nations people in his studio, in communities on the coast and en route to the gold fields. These images were published as engravings in books and illustrated papers, and they appeared annually in the mission reports of the Church of England. But mainly they were purchased alongside landscape

Shaft entrance to Neversweat Tunnel Claim, Williams Creek, about 1868. Frederick Dally, albumen print. BCA A-00937

"views" for the Victorian photograph albums of visitors and residents. Photography was beyond the ability of all but a very few amateurs and professionals, so clients purchased these views for their collections. Dally also made sumptuous presentation albums. At the end of his life in 1914, several of these were sent to the provincial archives along with numerous loose prints, a guarantee that his legacy would be preserved.[16]

The artists of the early gold rushes created paintings and photographs true to "what they saw" but also based on what they felt. Edward M. Richardson and Frederick Whymper produced works brimming with adventure and topographic prowess. William G.R. Hind captured the opposing individuality and kinship of the miner. Sarah Crease painted the busy emerging settler society of the colonial capital, Victoria. Charles Gentile and Frederick Dally brought a new technology to picture making as gold-rush society was entering a new phase of industrial organization. The original works, such as those held in the BC Archives, are surely our most authentic and telling views into the "strange and wonderful" history of British Columbia's gold rushes. ⚒

Chief's grave at Chapman's Bar, about 1868. Frederick Dally, albumen print. BCA C-09270

INDIAN GRAVE ON CARIBOO ROAD, BELOW LYTTON.

Indian Grave on Cariboo Road, below Lytton, about 1868. S. Haberer, engraving, after Frederick Dally.
BCA PDP01777

ACKNOWLEDGEMENTS

I am grateful to past colleagues who have amassed an astounding collection of works of art and photographs, along with rich artist and photographer reference files. Dr. Kathryn Bridge provided valuable recommendations.

NOTES

1   Andrew Wilton and Anne Lyles, *The Great Age of the British Watercolours, 1750-1880* (Munich: Prestel), 1993, p. 27.

2   Berenice C. Gilmore, *Artists Overland: A Visual Record of British Columbia 1793–1886* (Burnaby Art Gallery), 1980, p. 13. Gilmore's "paintings of a formal kind" are works where imagination and arranged composition outweigh literal depiction.

3   Vancouver *Province*, 1927. A cabinet photograph was approximately 16.5 x 11.5 cm.

4   Library and Archives Canada, National Gallery, Art Gallery of Ontario, Toronto Public Library, Winnipeg Art Gallery and McCord Museum.

5   May Jo Hughes, *Hindsight: William Hind in the Canadian West* (Winnipeg Art Gallery), 2002, pp. 13–63. All further information about Hind is drawn from this source and from the works in the BC Archives collection.

6   Eleanor C. Smyth, *An Octogenarian's Reminiscences* (Letchworth, UK: publisher unknown), 1916, p. 81; also in Gilmore.

7   Dennis Reid, *A Concise History of Canadian Painting* (Toronto: Oxford University Press), 2012, pp. 66-70.

8   Two works in the BC Archives, both titled *Richfield, Williams Creek,* (PDP00102 and PDP00103) are very similar in composition and detail, but have different colour schemes.

9   Reid, p 46-47.

10 Cesare Marino, *The Remarkable Carlo Gentile: Pioneer Italian Photographer of the American Frontier* (Nevada City, California: Carl Mautz Publishing), 1998, pp. 5-16.

11 Helen Bergen Peters, *Painting During the Colonial Period in British Columbia, 1845–1871* (Victoria: Sono Nis Press), 1979, pp. 25 and 75.

12 See Sarah Lindley (Crease, Lady Crease) in *Dictionary of Canadian Biography*, biographi.ca/en/bio/lindley_sarah_15E.html.

13 Ibid.

14 Richard C. Mayne, *Four Years in British Columbia and Vancouver Island* (London: John Murray), 1862, p. 45.

15 The *carte de visite* was a standardized format of mounted photographic print about the size of a calling card. It was easy to mail and was widely collected and placed in specially-designed photograph albums.

16 Joan M. Schwartz, "Dally, Frederick (1838–1914)" in *Encyclopedia of Nineteenth Century Photography*, edited by John Hannavy (New York: Routledge), 2008, p. 377.

Chinese Foot Prints in the Fraser Gold Rush (1858–60)

Lily Chow

||||||||||||||||||||||||||||||||||||||||||||||||||

INTRODUCTION

IN LATE 1858 NAM SING joined the gold stampede at the Fraser Canyon but did not have much luck in gold panning. After a few months he poled a canoe north from Yale to reach the vicinity of Quesnel. On the west bank of the Quesnel River he started mining using a rocker. Luck was still not with him in finding gold, so he tilled the land nearby to start vegetable gardening and then sold his produce to the residents in Quesnel. Later on, he acquired more land for farming and ranching. In 1880 he married Sue Cook, a young girl who emigrated from Guangdong and travelled to Quesnel by stagecoach to meet him for the first time. Together they produced and raised 13 children. Besides vegetable gardening, he raised cattle and pigs in his ranch, and owned and operated a pack train to deliver his produce as well as other goods between Quesnel and Barkerville. Two of his sons, Kong and Him, were excellent horsemen and ranked the best freighters in the Cariboo driving cattle from Ashcroft to Barkerville. In the early 1900s Nam Sing established a grocery store on Highway 26 near Wells, which was mainly manned by his children and grandchildren.

— Nam Sing family account[1]

IN 1858 the discovery of gold in the Fraser Canyon attracted many people of different nationalities, including the Chinese, to immigrate to New Caledonia – then the name of British Columbia. This influx of gold prospectors and miners started the Fraser gold rush in earnest. Uncovering individual names and stories of Chinese miners, such as Nam Sing, is difficult because the written record is sparse. Historians are making inroads by using digitized newspapers and government records, consulting genealogy websites, and connecting with family descendants in an effort to locate personal perspectives or, at the very least, reveal personal names. The Chinese segment of gold rush society has been understudied, and under-recognized in historical writing yet these people were integral to the shared experience of those thousands of gold seekers who ended up far from home searching for wealth and the opportunity to better themselves. I attempt here to trace in the records of the day the presence of Chinese, either as prospectors and miners or as businessmen and service providers, in the Fraser gold rush.

Accounting for gold: A Chinese brass scale, two types of weights used by Chinese merchants who operated stores throughout the gold fields and an account book listing gold dust brought to Victoria by Chinese miners.
Art Gallery of Greater Victoria SC854.1-50; RBCM 984.12.7 a-i; BCA K/EA/C43

THE ARRIVALS OF THE CHINESE IMMIGRANTS

THE DISCOVERY OF GOLD on the Fraser River reached the ears of Chinese prospectors and miners in California. Immediately, they joined the American miners in the gold stampede. On April 25, 1858, the steamship *Commodore* brought in 450 passengers to Fort Victoria. The arrivals included 30 Chinese from California – presumably Ah Hong was one of them. He then travelled north to check out the mining prospects. Upon his return to California, he reported to his fellow miners that gold along the Fraser River could be found by the "bucketful".[2] Within a month, San Francisco's Hop Kee & Company made arrangements to send a shipment of merchandise, including provisions and mining equipment, north for the Chinese gold seekers. On May 18, 1858, the *San Francisco Bulletin* reported the first instance of gold seekers coming not just from the California fields but from China:

Already the heads of the different Chinese companies in this State [California] are making arrangements to ship their countrymen among us [to Victoria]. We have ample news of what is doing in China by a merchant vessel, which came in this morning, making the passage in fifty days from Hong Kong. She brings a crowd of Chinamen who will no doubt find their way to the north.

On June 3, 1858, the *Victoria Gazette* reported that a group of 300 Chinese arrived in Victoria on board the *Caribbean* and "a batch of celestials has landed on the mainland from the Oregon via the Columbia".[3] In July 10 the same newspaper informed that a "great number of passengers arriving at the Fraser by the dozen of river boats are Chinamen".[4]

But not all the Chinese arrivals were miners; some of them were merchants looking for business opportunities in Fort Victoria. Ah Sou, a well known Chinese merchant in San Francisco, was reported "making arrangements to facilitate a heavy immigration of his countrymen to the new El Dorado of the North".[5]

THE CHINESE GOLD SEEKERS

THE CHINESE PROSPECTORS AND MINERS who landed in Victoria usually then boarded one of the sternwheelers – such as the *Enterprise, Sea Bird, Maria, Douglas* or the Hudson's Bay Company

steamer *Otter* – to sail across the Straight of Georgia to Fort Langley. Some would disembark and walk the trail leading to Harrison Lake and then continue on foot to Lillooet. Others came by sternwheelers up the Fraser to Fort Hope or via canoes to Yale, head of navigation on the Fraser.[6] A few Chinese gold seekers reached the gold fields overland from Oregon via the Columbia River, and others trekked along the trails from Whatcom (Bellingham) in Washington State to the Fraser regions.[7] Often they relied on Aboriginal people to guide them to the various gold fields.

By late 1858 about 300 Chinese immigrants had ventured to Tranquille Creek in Kamloops to pan for gold[8] and many were on their way to Lytton. These Chinese gold seekers from California, Oregon and Washington were soon joined by their countrymen who had emigrated from Guangdong and Hong Kong.

Miner using a rocker, a device that uses water to separate gold particles from sand and gravel. The basic design of a rocker: a large rectangular wooden box with one side open and no top cover; a series of ridges on the inside of the box's bottom; a wooden drawer with a handle and a metal sieve base fitted into the top of the box; the box is supported by either two curved strips of wood, like the rockers on a cradle, or four small wheels. To use a rocker, the miner shovelled dirt and gravel into the wooden drawer and added water. He pushed the rocker back and forth by the handle, and the oscillating motion washed away the sand and fine particles, leaving the gold particles trapped behind the ridges across the bottom of the box. Frederick Dally photograph, about 1868. BCA A-00353

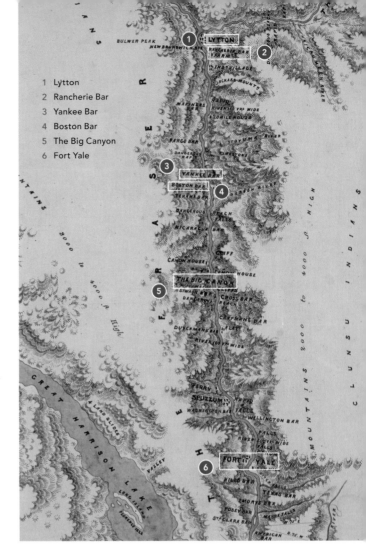

This map shows the locations of Lytton, the Big Canon, Fort Yale and a few sand bars where Chinese miners worked for gold. Adapted from Richard Charles Mayne, *Sketch Map of Port of British Columbia*, 1859. BCA CMC 187

1 Lytton
2 Rancherie Bar
3 Yankee Bar
4 Boston Bar
5 The Big Canyon
6 Fort Yale

Travelling on foot, the Chinese gold seekers had a special way of carrying their belongings to the gold fields. They carried their loads with a wooden pole 1.5 to 2 metres long. They fastened a canvas sack containing their mining gear, a tent and clothing with cords at one end of the pole, and the cooking utensils and provisions at the other. Then they balanced the pole on their shoulders and carried their loaded sacks to the claims. This was economical, because they only had to pay the native guide for leading them to the gold fields, not to pack supplies. Once they reached their destination, they pitched their tents and lost no time prospecting or digging and mining for gold. They were placer miners who used either a pan or a rocker or both to wash away river gravel to find gold particles.[9]

MISPERCEPTIONS AND CONFLICTS IN THE FRASER GOLD RUSH

MOST WHITE MINERS, when they could not find any more gold nuggets on their claim would abandon it to find another. But Chinese miners worked on claims meticulously, sifting through dirt and sand to trap the tiny specks of gold dust and flakes. They took over abandoned claims and worked them for what might be left behind. This practice was misinterpreted by newspaper reporters who intimated that the Chinese miners had jumped the claims of white miners and so stolen gold from the claim's rightful owners.[10]

The *Victoria Gazette* provides some of the most consistent evidence of this anti-Chinese sentiment and on contemporary western attitudes to Chinese (and indigenous) miners. For example: "This business of supplying the savages with liquor by the whites has found a counterpart

[the Chinese], who also furnished them with arms and ammunition … on the lower end of the Big Canon."[11] This was a matter of suspicion and assumption, as no proof had been found.

Indeed, there were struggles and clashes between indigenous peoples and the white miners in the Fraser Canyon. In August 21, 1858, the *Victoria Gazette* reported: "A fight had occurred at the Rancheria, where the Indians were killed and their encampment burnt. Ten Indians (one of whom was a chief) were killed and two whites, a man and a woman, from Hill's Bar died [during the fight]. Two companies, 150 men in each, were immediately formed at Fort Yale.… Serious trouble was apprehended." The miners then appointed Captain Snyder to take charge of the contingency. In his letter to the editor of the *Victoria Gazette*, Captain Snyder wrote: "It is said that the Chinese on a bar close by are in league with the savages.… All miners have left the river between Big Canon and the Fork [Lytton] on account of these disturbances."[12] Prior to any military actions, Captain Snyder and his men went to interrogate the Chinese miners on China Bar to learn if they had supplied firearms to indigenous peoples, and the Chinese miners denied having sold or supplied such ammunition. Snyder then asked the Chinese miners to leave their claims, as a battle between the white miners and First Nations would soon take place. The Chinese could return to their claims when the war was over.[13] Fortunately, Nlaka'pamux Chief David Spintlum (CexpentlEm) successfully intervened, preventing the war.[14]

CHINESE MINERS ARRIVE IN LYTTON

IN APRIL 6, 1860, Gold Commissioner Henry Ball wrote to the British Colonial Secretary: "Mining season has commenced.… Great numbers of Chinamen are daily arriving in these lower districts, and locating themselves as miners on the different bars, and have shown themselves a peaceful and orderly disposed class of people."[15] In the 1860–62 mining records, numerous Chinese miners had registered their claims. Here is an example of a claim statement:

> White Rock Bar, Lytton, May 28th, 1860
> This day, seven Chinamen, 1682; 1998; 1699; 1700; 4014; 4012; 4013, have recorded their right of 7 claims on White Rock Bar or Flat adjoining the claims of George King surveying downstream. Size of claims 100 feet square, Flat about 2 miles north of Creek.
> Possession has taken in May 27, 1860.
> Numbers [listed] are the same as those appear in their Free Miners Certificates.
> Signed: H.M. Ball

For reasons unconfirmed, most probably the language barrier, Chinese names were not recorded in most claim statements, only their Free Miners Certificate or licence numbers listed. But even without their names, the archival records show how many miners worked the Fraser each year. For instance, Henry Ball's ledgers of 1860 to 1863 for the vicinity of Lytton list Chinese claims and the number of Chinese miners in each claim. The transcription on page 86 is from the original document.

The total number of 183 indicates only those who had registered and paid licence fees for their claims in 1860. It does not include those who made no specific claim, such as those working independently on the shores of the creeks and streams nearby. Ball complained that "[those who] work with rockers, and travel from point to point do not take out their mining licences, as there is no claim in the Act compelling them to do so. A great loss to the revenue is occasioned."[17] Also, this list does not include the names of any Chinese miners who purchased claims from white miners. Transfer of ownership was not recorded by the gold commissioner. Here is an example of transference of mining claim:

> Transfer: Upper Yankee Flat
> This day Houn Chinaman No.1303 has recorded his right to a claim belonging to Louis Knight P. 281, and transferred by purchase to Houn as per bill of sale. Date: May 10th, 1860.[18]

In some places more than four people jointly staked their claims, and according to the mining records, they were listed as members of Chinese mining companies. For instance, Ah Chong was the head of the company in China Flat (July 30) and Ah Fou in Ah Fou Flat. Places such as China San Flat, China Eyed Flat (just north of Lytton on the Thomson River)[19], Assim Flat and others could each have covered a large area, as they were recorded more than once within a month by different groups of Chinese miners. Ball's records reveal that Chinese miners were located on the

NAMES OF CLAIMS	NUMBERS OF CHINESE MINERS	POSSESSION DATE
White Rock Bar	7	May 28
Canyon Flat	3	May 28
Below Ranchine Flat[16]	9	May 28
Ranchine Flat	3	May 28
Ranchine Flat: West Bank	4	May 30
Yankee Flat	2	June 8
12 Mile Flat	3	June 9
Opposite 21 Mile Flat	4	June 10
Flat; west bank of Fraser River	5	June 10
½ mile below Spring Bar	3	June 11
2 miles north of Kanaka Bar	6	June 30
Lower Yankee Flat	2	July 2
Assim Flat; 3 miles below Murderer's Bar	4	July 14
China San Flat; 3 miles south of 4 Mile House	4	July 21
China San Flat	10	July 24
China San Flat	4	July 24
China San Flat	3	July 12
Flat behind Rancheni Flat West bank	6	July 15
China Eyed Flat	2	July 25
China Eyed Flat	4	July 25
Assim Flat	3	July 26
Assim Flat	9	July 26
Ah Quee Flat	3	July 28
East bank Fraser opposite Last Chance Flat	5	July 30
China Flat	14	July 30
Assim Flat	2	August 5
Scotch Flat	3	August 6
Ah Quee Flat	1	August 7
Ah Fou Flat	10	August 8
China Flat	14	August 8
Task's Bar	2	August 11
China Flat	8	August 11
Assim Flat	1	August 12
North end of Wept Bar	2	August 18
Bank of Thompson River	4	August 21
Last Chance Flat	8	September 3
½ mile below Spring Flat	3	September 13
South of Cameron's Bar	3	October 29
TOTAL NUMBER	**183**	

"different flats on both sides of the Fraser, principally between Boston Bar and the Forks…. They are yielding $6.00 per head [per day] … most of the best claims at present are worked by Chinamen."[20] According to the times, this indicates a good rate of return. The Chinese miners were doing well in the vicinity of Lytton.

MOVING NORTH ALONG THE FRASER TO THE CARIBOO

IN JULY 1861 news about the discovery of gold in the Cariboo reached the miners in the Fraser Canyon. Henry Ball wrote to the government agent in Victoria with the information he had received. "Already at Antler Creek, a town as large as Lytton has sprung up, and the excitement and business there equal the excitements of the mining town in the early days of California."[21] His report was substantiated by notices and letters printed in the *British Colonist*. Many white miners left their claims on the lower Fraser and moved north along the river until they arrived in the new gold towns of Antler, Keithley, Richfield and Williams Creek in the Cariboo. The migrations of gold miners to the Cariboo indicate the ending of the Fraser gold rush.

In addition to the Cariboo, miners ventured east and south to Similkameen, Dog Creek and Granite Creek on the search and following rumours. Although some Chinese miners followed the footsteps of the white miners to these areas, many stayed behind and worked on abandoned claims along the Fraser, as they were certain that the white miners had left gold flakes and dust in the tailings. The presence of Chinese on the lower Fraser is substantiated in the official government documents kept at Hope between 1861 and 1862. In this instance, officials wrote down the names of several hundred Chinese gold seekers. These names give individuality and enable further research.

NOT EVERYONE WAS A GOLD SEEKER

NOT ALL THE CHINESE MINERS continued chasing the glittering metal. Those who realized that gold mining might not be a profitable enterprise took up other occupations such as working as labourers in road construction, in farmlands and ranches, and as packers.

For the miners to reach the gold fields, bridges and roads had to be built. In late 1858 the Royal Engineers supervised the construction of the first wagon road from Port Douglas to Lillooet. This alternative route to the upper Fraser River employed about 500 men of different nationalities, including some Chinese and Hawaiians, for its construction.[22] Another wagon road, the Cariboo Wagon Road from Yale to Barkerville, was built in 1862. These two important roads facilitated movement of people and supplies. Pack trains sped up transportation of passengers and delivery of goods to the interior and made it possible to provide support services for the miners who created towns in which merchants established saloons, restaurants, general and grocery stores, laundry shops and bath houses. Sawmills and lumber companies also emerged as the demand for timber increased. Wood was required to build bridges over rivers, streams and creeks so that miners could reach their claims. Flumes and rocker boxes and cribbing for tunnels all required wood, as did cabins, stores, churches, and town boardwalks. Chinese were employed as cooks in some sawmills, and possibly also as labourers.

Some pre-empted lands from the government for vegetable gardening and settled down in Yale, Hope, Lytton and Lillooet where they started small businesses such as grocery stores, laundry shops and restaurants. Others worked for the residents in these villages, chopping firewood and carrying water from nearby streams and rivers. A few even ventured to pack for miners and travellers to the Cariboo and the Similkameen. During 1861 no fewer than six Chinese at Lytton took out trading licences as packers.[23]

Below is a record of the Chinese people who acquired land in Lytton and its vicinity for vegetable gardening, information gathered from Henry Ball's ledgers from 1862 to 1865:

RECORDS OF FREE MINERS & STOREKEEPER OCCUPYING CROWN LAND AS GARDENERS AND RESIDENCE[24]

DATE	NAME	OCCUPATION	LOCALITY
1862, May 31	Ah Yung	Storekeeper	Situated on the Bench above the corner of the Wagon Road near the town of Lytton, measuring 61 yards from stump mining easterly thence northerly 66 yards. Plot for garden
1863, Mar 10	Ah Song	Free miner	About 2 acres opposite Court House for garden purposes
1863, Apr 30	Four Chinamen	Free miner	About 5 acres for garden purposes. Situated behind the Big Bar right bank of the Fraser River extending from the ravine and running north alongside the bench to the ravine near a little stream
1863, May 12	Ah Lchut	Free miner	Garden Plot: near China Flat, about 5 acres in the neighbourhood of M. Wha's house
1863, May 12	A Long & Ah Ching	Free miner	Garden plot near Spring Flat, west bank of the Fraser River about 3 acres on the mine side of the bench
1863, Oct 23	Ah Soup	Free miner	Garden plot about 5 acres south of garden plot of Ah Pow, opposite mouth of Thompson River
1864, May 19	Ah Sot	Free miner	5 acres on the bench on the opposite side of the Fraser at the mouth of the Thompson, for making hay
1864, May 23	Wai Chong	Free miner	5 acres for a garden on Spring Flat north of his claim (mining)
1864, Sept 7	Chung Lah & Ah Quan	Free miner	10 acres situated on Yankee Flat back from river, under mountain for garden purpose

DATE	NAME	OCCUPATION	LOCALITY
1864, Sept 19	Kum Sing	Free miner	5 acres situated about 2 miles below the sawmill for a garden above his claim
1864, Oct 19	Ah Kum	Free miner	5 acres for a garden plot near New Brunswick Creek, just above their claim near the ditch running from New Brunswick Creek
1864, Oct 26	Ah Lok	Free miner	5 acres for garden plot on Yankee Flat, back from river under mountain. Near the 2 claims of Chung Fat and Ah Quai
1864, Nov 2	Kum Sing (different person)	Free miner	5 acres for a garden on a flat west bank of Fraser near Lytton. Opposite the lunchion claim on the east bank
1864, Nov 14x	Man Kung	Free miner	5 acres situated on the Fraser between the mouth of Yankee Creek and a ditch running from the said creek on to the claim, short distance up stream
1864, Nov 14	Ah Lcheng & Ah Fook	Free miner	6 acres on Cameron Flat about 150 yards from their claims between the ditch and the Fraser
1864, Dec 19	Ah Pow	Free miner	5 acres for a garden on China Flat where the Blacksmith shop about 2 miles from Lytton
1865, Jan 25	Ah Fook	Free miner	3 acres for a garden above recorded claim
1865, Jan 25	Ah Sue	Free miner	1 acre about 300 yards north of above claim
1865 Jan 30	Shin Ho	Free miner	5 acres for a garden adjoining his claims on Mooron Bar, this side of the Fraser River
1865, Mar 18	Fok Ick	Free miner	5 acres for a garden on a bench in the angle formed by Dallas Creek and Fraser River, not to interfere with Indians
1865, Mar 22	Ing Tong	Free miner	5 acres for a garden contiguous to the above record

No records of payments for these lands are found in the ledger. Some Chinese, however, applied for trading licences to start their small businesses. Such licences were only valid for three months, after which they had to renew them. In Lytton, ten Chinese had applied for licenses for operating some stores, the nature of which was not disclosed; two for blacksmith business; one for a butcher shop; two for boat (presumably canoes) transportation; and fifteen for packing business.[25] Fook You on Chinese Flat was the last Chinese name in the mining record in 1873.

RACE RELATIONS

CHINESE IN THE GOLD RUSH kept to themselves, working alone or with other Chinese gold seekers. Their businesses were separate and distinct, often supplying infrastructure needs, goods and services to westerners yet remaining socially separate. We are hampered by a lack of references to social interactions in the writings of the western gold seekers and colonial society generally. Cultural differences, language and religion all played a part in Chinese marginalization. Racist attitudes by whites towards Chinese led to misunderstanding and misinformation.

But Chinese migrants shared this separateness with First Nations. They were treated with disrespect, not unlike that experienced by the Nlaka'pamux people, by American miners all along the Fraser. It seemed natural, then, that Chinese and Aboriginal people might become allies, might see each other as sharing the hostility received from the whites. References to interactions between the Chinese and aboriginal people are found in the newspapers of the time. When conflicts occurred between some American miners and the Nlaka'pamux, the Chinese miners in China Bar were accused of helping the natives in the preparation of Canyon War.[26] This assertion demonstrates the positive relationship between First Nations and the Chinese miners, although the role of the Chinese miners in the Canyon War has yet to be ascertained.

Another incident substantiates the good relationship between the First Nations and the Chinese gold miners. On March 21, 1862, the *British Colonist* reported that a native man and four Chinese were buried alive by a snow avalanche at McCrea's Lake, a mining locality eight kilometres north of Yale. These five miners lived together in a log cabin abandoned by white miners and worked together on a bar panning for gold. On the day of the accident, the native man saw an immense mass of snow detach from the mountain and slide down at great speed toward them while they were mining with a rocker near the water's edge. He gave an alarm to his co-workers, who turned to see the massive wave of snow coming at them. All of them fled, but before they could reach a place of safety the avalanche was upon them, burying them alive[27].

CONCLUSION

AT THE BEGINNING OF THE GOLD RUSH, Governor James Douglas and Hudson's Bay Company officials at Fort Victoria noted the arrival of Chinese immigrants in their correspondence and journal entries. The presence of Chinese gold miners was also noticed in the gold country. But few accounts exist about how these Chinese miners lived their lives in a foreign land. To a certain extent, they were treated as aliens, because they looked strange: they wore different clothing and braided their hair into a queue. The language barrier and cultural differences could be other factors that hindered communications between the Chinese and other people in the community.

The Chinese miners, businessmen and labourers in the gold rush certainly contributed to the economy, to the growth and development of British Columbia generally and also to Victoria and Barkerville and the smaller communities along the Cariboo Wagon Road. But the Chinese prospectors, miners, merchants and service providers have not yet been accorded equal treatment in reconstructing this important period in British Columbia's history. Historians have just begun to scratch the surface in tracing the Chinese within the gold rush to rectify this imbalance in our knowledge. This account is not exhaustive because the sources of information are limited to reports from early newspapers, government records, journals and books written by scholars and historians. My intention is to guide future research by including examples of where official records provide primary evidence and facilitate further investigation. ⚒

Axe head. During the gold rush, Hudson's Bay Company blacksmiths sold hand-forged tools as fast as they could make them. RBCM 965.186.1

ACKNOWLEDGEMENTS

I would like to thank Professor Jack Lohman for approving this article, Dr Kathryn Bridge for her encouragement and guidance in reviewing the writing, Don Bourdon for his great efforts in finding maps and images for illustrations, and Gerry Truscott for his meticulous editing and judicious comments.

NOTES

1 Lily Chow, *Sojourners in the North* (Prince George: Caitlin Press), 1996, pp. 54–55.

2 "BC Chinese made vast contribution", Vancouver *Sun* Centennial Edition, 1957.

3 *Victoria Gazette*, June 30, 1858, p.2.

4 Ibid., July 10, 1858, p. 2.

5 Ibid., July 17, 1858, p. 3.

6 *Victoria Gazette*, July 21, 1858, p. 2.

7 Chow, *Sojourners in the North*, p. 12.

8 "First Chinese here in 1858", Kamloops *Daily Sentinel*, December 19, 1970, p. 9.

9 Lily Chow, *Chasing Their Dreams* (Prince George: Caitlin Press), 2000, p. 3.

10 *Victoria Gazette,* July 10, 1858, p. 2.

11 Ibid., August 14, 1858, p. 2.

12 Ibid., August 21, 1858, p. 3.

13 Ibid., August 21, 1858, p. 4. (Found under "Indian Difficulties", a letter from Captain Snyder.)

14 Hauka, Donald, *McGowan's War* (Vancouver: New Star Books), 2003, pp. 89-91.

15 BC Government Agency, Correspondence, Lytton, April 6, 1860.

16 Andrew D. Nelson and Michael Kennedy's *Fraser River Gold Mines and their Place Names: a Map from Hope to Quesnel Forks,* 2012 (cartographic material located in the main library of the University of Victoria, G3512F79H2), marks this sand bar as the Rancheria Flat. So did the map produced by Royal Navy Lieut. R.C. Mayer in 1859. But the Manual of Records and Transfers, Lytton 1869–72 registered this bar as Ranchine Flat.

17 Henry Ball's Ledger, March 1, 1861.

18 Manual of Records and Transfers, Lytton,1860–62, GR 252, vol. 12, file 2.

19 Numerous Chinese claims listed in this essay can be found in Nelson and Kennedy's map, *Fraser River Gold Mines and their Place Names*, 2012.

20 BC Government Agency, Correspondence, Lytton, May 10, 1860.

21 Ibid., July 4, 1861.

22 A. Charles Banks, *British Columbia and Sir James Douglas K.B.B.,* The Newcomer Society in North America, n.d., p. 10.

23 Roderick J. Barman, "Packing in British Columbia". *The Journal of Transport History* 21:2 (September 2000), p. 148. **Barman states that** in 1867 Kwong Lee & Co. had a train of 35 mules working out of Yale, then the starting point of the wagon road to the Cariboo mines.

24 Mining, trading and garden records, Lytton, GR 833.

25 Ibid.

26 *Victoria Gazette*, August 14 and 21, 1858. The events leading to the Canyon War were also reported by a special agent of the United States in March 3, 1859, under the title "Fraser Gold Rush, Vancouver's Island and British Columbia: Message from the President of the United States Communicating" (CHIM 42565).

27 *British Colonist*, March 31, 1862 p. 3.

辦一生意係個條僱人幸嘉金
方停到到二嘆人年九
僱民安置其食用十二英尺二英尺橫地方式
隱地搭蓉用照一直上景在地方式
開搭式律例
坂涛後共立該所
此船位載長八百五十二尺以
立該船載行八百五十二尺以內
坂單位銀或留五年以
為據
員別

年
月
日

Trans-Pacific Gold Mountain Trade

Traces of Material Culture from British Columbia's Gold Rush

Tzu-I Chung

||||||||||||||||||||||||||||||||||||||||||||||||||

And Australia and California and the Pacific Ocean!
The new citizen of the world won't be able to
comprehend how small our world was.

– Karl Marx to Joseph Weydenmeyer, 25 March 1852[1]

THE 19TH-CENTURY GOLD RUSHES played a key role not only in shaping British Columbia but also in starting "the Pacific century" and transforming the Pacific from a peripheral zone to "a nexus of world trade".[2] Gold seekers from many parts of Europe, the Americas and Asia followed the gold trail around the Pacific Rim. Even though only a few of the gold seekers became wealthy, the increased supply of gold stimulated global trade and investment and brought profits to some merchants engaged in the trans-Pacific trade.[3] In British Columbia the gold rush initiated the first major Chinese settlement to Canada. This article provides a brief account of the early Chinese pioneers' stories within the regional, national and trans-Pacific context. First-person accounts of Chinese gold seekers are rare, but the activities of merchants can be traced through material culture studies and archival research.

EARLY TRANS-PACIFIC CROSSINGS AND NINETEENTH-CENTURY GOLD RUSHES

SOME TRANS-PACIFIC TRADE existed before the gold rush. In 1757 the Qing emperor Chien-Lung banned maritime activities in general, and confined foreign trade to Canton, today's Guangzhou City, the capital of Guangdong Province. In 1780 British and American traders began shipping fur and lumber from Nootka Sound on Vancouver Island to Hong Kong, Macao and Canton. Among the early traders was John Meares (1756–1809), a British fur trader, who made the first of several voyages between the Pacific Northwest and Asia in 1786. According to his journal, in 1788 he sailed with 50 Chinese "handicraft-men" and sailors to Nootka Sound, where they were believed to have built the sloop *North West America*, and Nootka Sound became a base for trade between the Pacific Northwest coast and Guangzhou and Macao.[4]

After winning the Opium War (1839–42), Great Britain forced China to open five ports and cede Hong Kong Island in the Treaty of Nanking (1842). Canton's role as the exclusive port for foreign trade laid a foundation for spreading the news of gold mountains, pushing emigration and expanding trade in the pan-Pacific area. Along the very long Chinese coast, the Pearl River Delta (including Canton and its surrounding counties) became the major place of origin for Chinese migrants.

Launching the *North West America* at Nootka Sound, Vancouver Island. BCA A-02688

Rose Dew Wine bottle.
RBCM 2002.47.51

This densely populated area was ravaged by civil wars, including the Taiping Rebellion, and natural catastrophes such as famine and flood, resulting in hardships and exacerbating poverty. Significantly, the opening of new ports allowed Hong Kong Island to rise quickly from a fishing village to a major port for oceanic trade.[5] As a result of that development, Canton and Hong Kong served as the main centres in China for the trade that followed a series of gold rushes around the Pacific: California (1849), Australia (1851), British Columbia (1858) and New Zealand (1861).

While difficulties in southern China served as a major "push" factor for Chinese migration, the "Gold Mountain Dream" ignited by the gold rushes became the "pull" factor. Originally, the Chinese term "gold mountain" (金山, pronounced as *gum saan* in Cantonese) meant gold mines or gold fields, but in the 19th century, it came to mean the land of promise and opportunities of wealth. After gold was found in California, San Francisco became the Gold Mountain City (金山大埠); in Australia, Melbourne became officially New Gold Mountain City (新金山); in 1858 British Columbia's Fraser River became the next Gold Mountain, and Victoria became a main entrepôt. In Guangdong and Hong Kong, Gold Mountain became a popular image. The gold seekers – that is, the sojourner/guests (金山客, *gum saan haak*) – were highly-sought-after husbands, sons-in-law or business partners.[6] The Gold Mountain Dream did not fade even in the early 20th century. It has informed the name of many past and recent art and literary works about the 19th century[7] and even appeared in the poems Chinese immigrants wrote on the walls while in detention at the federal immigration building in Victoria.

The daily needs of the Chinese gold seekers – from food and clothing to education and entertainment – shaped the composition of the gold mountain trade,[8] and created and maintained what Philip Kuhn has called a "cultural, social and economic corridor".[9] Their consumption of made-in-China goods during the gold rush and long after, contributed to trans-Pacific trade and the prosperity of Chinese merchants.[10] But this choice also contributed to the non-Chinese perception of Chinese as sojourners in the host countries.

The history collection of the Royal BC Museum contains a number of examples of trade goods that supplied migrants' needs. One is a liquor bottle for rose dew wine made in Hong Kong. Similar liquor bottles have been found throughout British Columbia and other areas around the Pacific Rim reached by Chinese migrants. The Pearl River Delta also exported the mud silk outfits to Chinese labourers overseas. These garments are made of a special kind of mud-treated silk designed originally for the warm, humid weather of that area.[11] The inside of the garment was mud-coloured and the outside black, designed for both summer and "hardwearing", and characterized by durability, comfort, water resistance and being easy to clean.[12] Although the climate of British Columbia was cooler and less humid than that of the Pearl River Delta, the fact

A produce
pedlar's clothes,
pole and baskets.
RBCM 996.7.1
996.7.2

that the Royal BC Museum has one of the largest known existing bi-coloured mud silk collections from local communities in the world indicates that the garment was widely worn here.[13]

BRITISH COLUMBIA'S GOLD RUSH AND THE CHINESE IN VICTORIA

IN THE SPRING OF 1858 news of gold in the Fraser Canyon transformed Fort Victoria from a quiet fur trade outpost of the Hudson's Bay Company into a booming town. Hop Kee & Company of San Francisco played an instrumental role in the first wave of Chinese to Victoria.[14] On June 24, 1858, it commissioned Allan Lowe & Company in San Francisco to ship 300 Chinese men and 50 tons of merchandise to Victoria at the cost of $3500.[15] Most men departed for the gold fields soon after arriving. Throughout the summers of 1858 and 1859 Chinese continued to arrive from the United States; by 1859 clipper ships were bringing hundreds of Chinese immigrants directly from Hong Kong. The Royal BC Museum and Archives collection contains samples from a stack of bilingual tickets issued to Chinese men and boys for passage on the *Maria* from Hong Kong to Victoria in 1865. The Chinese names of the passengers are written in Chinese calligraphy on the upper left corner. This rare archival evidence reveals that conditions on these trans-Pacific voyages were harsh, with only one meal per day and a sleeping space of only 14 inches (35.5 cm) for each of the 316 Chinese passengers (in contravention of the Chinese Passengers Act of 1855).

Due to the discrimination the Chinese faced in California, three Chinese merchants who were among the first wave of Chinese to arrive in Victoria – Loo Chuck Fan, Wong Tien Lui and Chang Tsoo – purchased land at the edge of Fort Victoria on the other side of a ravine (which was later filled in and is now Johnson Street). This practice

of creating a distinct Chinatown a bit separate from the main community was repeated later in the gold rush town of Barkerville. In Victoria, the merchants set up stores – Tai Soong & Company, Kwong Lee & Company and Yan Woo Sang & Company – and built wooden huts as tenement houses for the labourers they recruited in San Francisco and later China. When Victoria was incorporated as a city in 1862, 300 of its citizens (about six per cent of the city's population) were Chinese. This percentage changed constantly through seasons and with new arrivals, as some miners wintered in Victoria and newcomers either passed through Victoria briefly before setting out for gold fields or stayed for jobs mainly in the city's service sectors.

Unlike Californians, colonial British Columbians were relatively tolerant of the Chinese at first. Few whites perceived the Chinese as a threat to their well-being. Some regarded the Chinese as useful or valuable members of the community who shared the goal of making money and whose presence might lead to the growth of a profitable trans-Pacific trade.[16] Indeed, Chinese labourers provided useful services as laundrymen, servants, barbers, tailors, cobblers or other tradesmen, or as cooks, domestic servants, market gardeners and washmen for the non-Chinese population.

By colonial law the Chinese had access to legal rights.[17] For example, in 1862, when Esquimalt (a port adjacent to Victoria) grew to a point where it wanted a resident police force independent from that of Victoria, three Chinese residents were among the "householders, Traders, Hotel Keepers, and residents" of the Town of Esquimalt who signed a petition to Governor James Douglas of Vancouver Island.

The Chinese community interacted with all walks of society. Lee Chang (or Chong), manager of Kwong Lee & Co., was an early model of an intercultural personality. He was well known by the non-Chinese public as "Kwong Lee", even

Ad in the Victoria newspaper, the *British Colonist*, 1864.

though he was not the owner of the firm. A British traveller described him as: "A gentleman of most polite manners and very intelligent. Speaks English fluently in ordinary conversation. Free from Yankee twang and slang."[18] In August 1858 a newspaper reported that Lee Chang, "a well-known and respectable commission merchant," had acted as a court interpreter when a Chinese man was charged with selling liquor to a native Indian.[19] Lee Chang was one of the very few Chinese residents wealthy enough to have his family join him. On February 29, 1860, his wife and two children arrived in Victoria from San Francisco. Mrs Lee Chang (sometimes known as Mrs Kwong Lee) became the first Chinese woman to settle in Victoria.[20] Her presence and that of her children suggests that the Lee Chang family intended to be settlers, not sojourners.

Victoria's Chinese merchants also took leadership in speaking up for collective rights. Lee Chang represented the Chinese community before the government on March 7, 1860, when he and two other merchants went to see Governor James Douglas after hearing of a suggestion to impose a poll tax on Chinese immigrants.[21] According to historian David Tung-Hai Lee, "during Douglas's term [as governor ...] British subjects in Victoria mostly abused Chinese".[22] So when Douglas's successor, Arthur Kennedy, arrived in Victoria in April 1864, Lee Chang, Tong Kee and Chang Tsoo called on him to express their hope for the fair treatment of the Chinese population and to raise concerns about the government's plan to modify the colony's free-trade policy.[23] Based on the Chinese account, Governor Kennedy was friendly, maintained a positive relationship with, and enjoyed good reputation among Chinese communities during his term here that ended in 1866, and also during his term as the governor of Hong Kong.[24]

In the late 19th century, one of the main complaints against the Chinese presence was the perception that they were sojourners who contributed little to the local economy before moving on to another gold field or back to China.[25] But while many were sojourners, the examples of Lee Chang in British Columbia and of Chinese in Australia and New Zealand show that, in general, the gold rush migration pattern of the Chinese paralleled that of European settler communities along the Pacific Rim.[26]

The leading Chinese merchants, the owners of Kwong Lee and Tai Soong, made the city's Chinatown an influential economic centre in the trans-Pacific gold mountain trade. In their address to Governor Kennedy, Lee Chang and the others pointed out that active trade was taking place in the early 1860s, when large amounts of silk, tea, sugar and rice were imported from China, with the prospect of growing exportation of lumber, coal, minerals and fish to China from British colonies here.[27]

By 1862, eleven Chinese companies paid taxes under a local Trade License Ordinance. Kwong Lee, the largest company in Victoria second only to the Hudson's Bay Company, was assessed at £6500, while Tai Soong and Yan Woo Sang & Company were assessed in at £2000–6000.[28]

The Kwong Lee advertisement provides the clues to the historical trans-Pacific connections between Canton and Hong Kong and British Columbia.[29] Just as Kwong Lee operated its principal offices in Canton

Advertisement in the *First Victoria Directory and British Columbia Guide,* 1868.

and Hong Kong, as this image shows, the owners of Tai Soong & Co. located at 40–42 Cormorant Street (today's 550–556 Pandora Avenue, Victoria) also operated Tai Chuen Company in Hong Kong and Kwong San Tai Company in San Francisco.[30] Two or three times a year, Wong Tien Lui chartered a clipper to ship tons of dried goods and Chinese merchandise from Hong Kong to Victoria and then distributed the goods to Chinese stores in gold-mining towns on the mainland.[31]

Central to these merchants' activities were the brass scales that they imported from China to weigh gold and goods. While no complete scale from the 1850s or 1860s has apparently survived, bits and pieces found at various sites in British Columbia indicate that this type of scale was used. The weight pieces, big and small, are each engraved with Chinese characters of their weight by Chinese measurement. Well-preserved sets of this kind of weights, as well as other types of commonly used Chinese weights, are held in multiple collections throughout the province. While their shapes and sizes may vary from set to set (some in square shapes), these Chinese weights were designed to travel, so each piece fits into the next and, in turn, they are all packed into the largest one to form a compact set. The presence of this Chinese merchants' device at sites around the province suggests the far reach of the gold mountain trade.

The gold mountain trade reshaped a trans-Pacific network of migration and commerce. Within this growing network, Victoria (and later Vancouver), Hong Kong, Canton, San Francisco, and other Pacific ports served as the in-between places that sustained a vibrant flow of people, goods, funds, commercial intelligence, correspondence, and even dead bodies and bones.[32] Chinese migrants travelled back and forth across the Pacific through these ports that sometimes became their second homes. In British Columbia, Victoria served as the major port between Canada and Asia until the completion of the Canadian Pacific Railway and the establishment of its western terminus at Vancouver in 1887, when that city gradually took on that role. Nevertheless, as an "in-between place," Victoria long remained home to one of the largest Canadian-born Chinese populations until well into the 20th century.

The trans-Pacific network enabled Chinese to contribute much to the building of British Columbia. In the 1860s and 1870s, Chinese merchants and labourers were involved in many public projects, such as erecting telegraph poles, constructing the 607-kilometre Cariboo Wagon Road, building trails, digging canals and reclaiming wastelands. Opportunities for Chinese labourers increased after an 1862 smallpox epidemic decimated the First Nations population. At this time, gold was discovered much further north in the Cariboo at Williams Creek, which rapidly grew into the town of Barkerville. Victoria's Chinese merchants quickly took advantage of this new gold rush. By 1863 Chinese businesses were established including brothels, opium dens and restaurants, and about 4000 Chinese lived in the Cariboo.

The Kwong Lee advertisement further testifies to the role of Victoria, as an in-between place, connecting the interior of British Columbia to the trans-Pacific network. By 1868 the company had stores in Yale, Lillooet, Quesnelle Forks, Quesnel and Barkerville, among other gold rush towns. Both Kwong Lee and Tai Soong quickly developed a network of subsidiaries and agencies in all the gold rush towns of BC. They made, sold and delivered products and services. They operated transportation businesses, first with mules and later with wagons, up the Fraser River Valley and into the Cariboo.[33] A receipt survives that was issued for the transportation of gold dust belonging to Kwong Lee dated 1861. On the back of the receipt one can see the common Chinese business practice of the time: the receipt is summarized in Chinese calligraphy.

A unique artifact in the collection of the Quesnel Museum testifies to the special needs of the gold rush towns, whose wooden buildings were fire hazards. The September 20, 1866, issue of the *Cariboo Sentinel* reports a fire in a Chinese wash house in Barkerville. After a major fire on September 16, 1868, Barkerville quickly rebuilt itself. The Quesnel and District Museum and Archives has preserved a long, extendable Chinese fire pump with its original engraving showing that it was tailor-made by fire-pump specialist Zhang Fa Company (长 Long 发 Prosperous 号 Company) located on the east side of the city of Canton.

Extendable Chinese fire pump, left; detail above. (Pump courtesy of the Quesnel & District Museum and Archives.) 1955.14.1

OPIUM AND GOLD
IMPORTANT TRADE COMMODITIES

AMONG THE MERCHANDISE that drove the booming trans-Pacific trade was opium, an important commodity from the global British trade that was legal in Canada until 1908. The British had exported opium from India to China to offset trade deficit from Britain's importation of silk, tea and china. After China's defeat in the Opium Wars, opium became integrated into Chinese lives. Tai Soong & Co. was a leading opium manufacturer in British Columbia. Like other leading Chinese merchants, Tai Soong operated its own opium refineries in Victoria's Chinatown.[34] In the 1880s Victoria was North America's major centre for opium distribution. Many people, men and women, of diverse nationalities smoked opium.

The opium dens in Victoria and gold rush towns served both Chinese and non-Chinese customers. Its contribution to tax revenues may explain why the government at all levels were slow to close it down.[35] In 1865 a licence fee of $100 was imposed on each seller of smoking opium, which rose to $250 by 1886; at the same time, sellers of opium-containing patent medicines, all of them white, were exempted.[36] From 1868 to 1871 the duty on imported raw opium was 25 per cent.[37] From the perspective of trade, it was important for the regional economy. Along the Fraser River Canyon, pieces of old opium cans were still being found in the mid 20th century, but few people recognized them and most were lost. One opium can that was reconstructed from pieces dug along the Fraser River bears an engraving in Chinese on the lid that reads "Victoria's Tai Soong & Co.".

Victoria's Chinese merchants also dealt in gold dust. Tai Soong & Co. appears several times in an extant gold dust account book. This account book in Chinese calligraphy recorded the continuing gold mining activities from 1883 to 1903, as a legacy of the early gold rush after the 1860s. After 1868, as the gold fields petered out and many were abandoned, some Chinese persisted in looking for gold along the Fraser River.[38] Chinese thus became the majority population in many gold rush towns in the late 19th century. Although the gold rush was over, between 1881 and 1885 more than 15,000 Chinese worked on the construction of the Canadian Pacific Railway. After the railway was built, many Chinese returned to China or found work elsewhere. Some of them sought gold in the Fraser Canyon and found small quantities of it. As the account book shows, in some cases they remitted the money to China.[39] Tai Soong served as one

Chinese gold seekers arriving directly from China found it difficult to earn a living, so the need for social support grew. Most Chinese miners worked in groups, but white miners often drove them away from claims with better yields, forcing them to work in abandoned claims. They described this as "flipping through sand dump".[41]

Because of such problems,[42] the first Chinese organization was established in the gold fields – in 1863 at Barkerville. Originally it was a secret society in China called Hongmen. It refashioned itself in North America and adopted the Freemasons' icon while retaining the old-world hierarchy and rules. The Chinese Freemasons was then the only organization that protected the Chinese population, so most Chinese belonged. Although many other Chinese organizations have appeared since, the Freemasons remain an influential organization in Chinese-Canadian communities today. A small woodblock-printed book in Chinese characters is held at the Clinton Museum – the Chinese were long an important presence in Clinton.[43] The artifact, dated 1892, is an early edition of the Hongmen Society manual for members, rich in information about its founders and history. In particular, the book contains many colourful illustrations, exemplifying the advanced printing technology of 19th-century China and making

of the main agencies that handled these transactions. The continuity of gold mountain trade extended the trans-Pacific "corridors" from the gold rush era and transformed both the sending and receiving regions of these migrants for decades to come.

SOCIAL SUPPORT AND LIFE IN THE GOLD FIELDS

IN THE GOLD FIELDS Chinese pioneers could not always rely on legal protection, thus requiring them to establish their own network of social support. Between 1858 and 1860 Chinese miners, who aquired skills in California, could earn a reasonable income.[40] After 1860, however, as the gold bars were mined out and competition for the remaining gold increased, the inexperienced

Barkerville's Chinatown, 1946. Frank Swannell photograph; BCA I-33442

The presence of this old-world manual in Clinton alongside a white fan is intriguing. While educated Chinese men at that time commonly used white fans, the white fan (白紙扇) also symbolized a special rank and position in Hongmen, that of the think tank/main strategist advisor/financial officer of the society. The words on this particular white fan, *zhong-cheng tong-shen*, strongly convey values of a Chinese secret society: loyalty, earnestness and connection with spirits. The white fan and the manual illustrate the prominence of the Chinese Freemasons in the far corners of the New World.

In addition to the Freemasons' lodges, the Chinese built temples or joss houses in the gold rush towns.[45] In these early times many relied on religion for support and comfort. At special

it unique among other existing manuals. Chinese Freemasons' lodges were subsequently established in Quesnel, Quesnel Forks and other gold rush towns across the interior of British Columbia.[44] While a few other early manuals survived, the Clinton Museum's artifact is emblematic of a once-active, thriving community and demonstrates persistence of the old-world hierarchy and rules in that community.

Joss house or temple bells. RBCM 996.7.3

occasions such as Chinese New Year (the first day of the first month in the lunar calendar) or Hungry Ghost Festival (the fifteenth day on the eighth month in the lunar calendar), celebrations in gold rush towns often attracted non-Chinese residents too. A set of 19th-century temple bells from Williams Lake represent early religious practice in the gold fields. As the Chinese population grew, more clan associations established branches in the gold rush towns.

Across diverse cultures, gambling was a common entertainment in the gold fields, as well as in Victoria's Fan Tan Alley, which the Chinese referred to as "Bank Street", where wealthy merchants operated gambling dens. In Barkerville, archaeologists have discovered that fan-tan[46], dominos and card games were the three

Kau Chim, a Chinese fortune telling device and gambling game. For fortune telling the bamboo sticks are placed in the container. The container is shaken and the sticks that fall out provide an answer to a question. These sticks are also used to play White Pigeon Tickets, a gambling game similar to Keno. Grant Keddie collection. L12014

major gambling activities of Chinese in the early period.[47] Gambling, although considered one of the three evils of early Chinatowns, has today left an important legacy of material culture – game pieces from the Qing dynasty.

Early Chinese travellers across the Pacific relied upon their trans-Pacific connections and developed the China-Canada trade. British Columbia sent lumber, coal and fish to China, and imported rice, sugar and opium. After the Canadian Pacific Railway was completed, it carried all kinds of goods, especially tea and silk, from China to eastern North America.[48] Tracing the material culture reveals the impact of the gold mountain trade and of what Henry Yu fittingly calls "Cantonese Pacific",[49] across which the goods from the Pearl River Delta transformed lives around the Pacific Rim. These early pioneers contributed to a significantly transformative chapter in trans-Pacific and Chinese Canadian history and demonstrated that Chinese played far

A White Pigeon Ticket. RBCM R2063

more active roles in the Pacific world than simple labourers or sojourners.[50] Many of these early migrants settled here and helped shape the British Columbia and Canada of today. ⚒

NOTES

1   Henry Mayer, ed., *Marx, Engels, and Australia* (Melbourne: Cheshire), 1964, p. 105. Here Karl Marx referenced the 19th-century gold-rush travels that reached the far corners of the world and made the world seem much more accessible and smaller.

2   Elizabeth Sinn, *Pacific Crossing: California Gold, Chinese Migration, and the Making of Hong Kong* (Hong Kong University Press), 2013, p. 1.

3   Keir Reeves, "Tracking the Dragon Down Under: Chinese Cultural Connections in Gold Rush Australia, Aotearoa, and New Zealand", *Graduate Journal of Asia-Pacific Studies* 3:1 (2005), p. 51.

4   John Meares, *Voyages Made in the Years of 1788 and 1789 from China to the North West Coast of America* (Logographic Press), 1790.

5   See Sinn 2013.

6   Sinn 2013, p. 188.

7   For example, a film coproduced by Canada and China on the construction of the Canadian Pacific Railway is entitled "Iron Road" in English and "Gold Mountain" in Chinese.

8   See Appendix I in Sinn 2013, pp. 309-11. Hong Kong exports to San Francisco in 1849, in 23 vessels, 4,950 tons. The exported goods ranged from eggs, and soda water to paint and bricks.

9   See Philip Kuhn, *Chinese Among Others: Emigration in Modern Times* (Lanham, Maryland: Rowman and Littlefield), 2008, p. 46.

10   David Tung-Hai Lee, *Chinese Canadian History* (in Chinese). Vancouver: Canada Liberty Publishers, 1967, 66. My translation.

11   ShuHwa Lin, "Analysis of Two Chinese Canton Silks: Jiāo-chou and Xiang-yun-shā" (2008). *Textile Society of America Symposium Proceedings*. Paper 111. http://digitalcommons.unl.edu/tsaconf/111, accessed October 22, 2014; Abby Lillethun, "Black Silk, Brown Silk: China and

Beyond—Traditional Practice Meets Fashion" (2008). *Textile Society of America Symposium Proceedings.* Paper 110. http://digitalcommons.unl.edu/tsaconf/110, accessed October 22, 2014.

12   Lillethun 2008, pp. 3 and 10.

13   See Lin 2008 and Lillethun 2008, p. 6. The current largest known collection is the Costume Collection at the University of Hawai'i at Mānoa (UHM), also in the Pacific Rim. The American Museum of Natural History holds a large collection of solid black (not bi-coloured) mud-treated silks, which were originally collected in Shanghai. Thanks to the previous RBCM Collections Manager Charlene Gregg, conservation intern Kate Blair and Conservators Kjerstin Mackie and Colleen Wilson for the work in identifying this textile collection.

14   BC Archives MS 1053.

15   David Chuenyan Lai, *Chinatowns: Towns within Cities in Canada* (Vancouver: UBC Press), 1988, pp. 15-16.

16   Patricia E. Roy, *A White Man's Province: British Columbia Politicians and Chinese and Japanese Immigrants 1858–1914* (Vancouver: UBC Press), 1989, p. 5.

17   Roy 1989, pp. 6-7.

18   Walter B. Cheadle, *Cheadle's Journal of a Trip Across Canada, 1862–63* (Edmonton: Hurtig), 1971, p. 268.

19   *Daily Victoria Gazette,* Victoria, August 10, 1858.

20   *British Colonist,* Victoria, March 1, 1860.

21   *British Colonist,* Victoria, March 8, 1860.

22   Lee, 1967, pp. 85-6.

23   *British Colonist,* Victoria, April 5, 1864.

24   Lee, 1967, pp. 85-88. Based on this account, Kennedy's service as governor was very well-received by Chinese in Hong Kong.

25   This early perception persists today in North America. As Asian-American scholar Robert G. Lee explains, the common questions many Asian Americans (and Asian Canadians) get, "Where do you come from?... No, where do you really come from?" are based on the assumption that Asians are sojourners. But such assumptions could have extreme consequences. See Lee, *Orientals: Asian Americans in Popular Culture* (Philadelphia: Temple University Press), 1999, pp. ix–x.

26   Reeves 2005, 56.

27   *British Colonist,* Victoria, April 5, 1864.

28   Harry Con et al., *From China to Canada: A History of the Chinese Communities in Canada* (Toronto: McClelland and Stewart), 1982, p. 16.

29   *First Victoria Directory and British Columbia Guide* (Victoria: Edward Mallandaines), 1868, p. 77.

30   *A Commemorative Issue of the Grand Opening of the Yue Shan Society Building in Vancouver* (Vancouver: Yue Shan Society), 1949, Section 2, p. 2. Cited in David Chuenyan Lai, *Chinese Community Leadership: Case Study of Victoria in Canada* (Singapore: World Scientific Publishing), 2010, p. 52.

31   David Chuenyan Lai, *Chinese Community Leadership: Case Study of Victoria in Canada* (Singapore: World Scientific Publishing Co. Pte. Ltd.), 2010, 52-3.

32   Sinn 2013, p. 136. See also Hon Ming Yip, *The Tung Wah Coffin Home and Global Charity Network: Evidence and Findings from Archival Materials* (Hong Kong: Sanlian Shudian), 2009. Dr Yip studied the large-scope charitable service of shipping dead bodies and bones from overseas through Hong Kong to the hometowns of the deceased, a folk practice important for Chinese of the time. Dr Yip explained that from the US, the shipping went through various Pacific ports, whereas in Canada, Victoria was the only trans-Pacific port for this practice.

33   Con et al., 1982, p. 18.

34   Lai 2010, p. 52.

35   Lai 2010, p. 38.

36   David Chuenyan Lai, "Chinese Opium Trade and Manufacture in British Columbia, 1858–1908." *Journal of the West,* 38: 3, 1999, pp.21-26.

37   *Victoria City Directory* 1868, p. 2058. In *British Columbia City Directories 1860–1955* Online. http://www.vpl.ca/bccd/index.php/browse/title/1868/First_Victoria_Directory_2nd_Issue.

38   Lee 1967, p. 65.

39   BC Archives K/EA/C43.

40   Lee 1967, p. 73.

41   Lee 1967, pp. 63-64.

42   Lee 1967, pp. 63-64 and 73-76.

43   Initially it was the two American researchers, Drs Chuimei Ho and Ben Bronson, who first brought my attention to these two objects in the Clinton Museum. <http://www.cinarc.org/Freemasons.html#anchor_219>

44   See Lily Chow, *Sojourners in the North* (Prince George: Caitlin Press), 1996.

45   Lee 1967, 67. The word "joss" is a Pidgin English word originally from the Portuguese word *Dios,* meaning God. Many joss houses in gold rush towns housed shrines of ancestors or patron saints of different types of associations.

See David Chuenyan Lai, *The Forbidden City within Victoria: Myth, Symbol, and Streetscape of Canada's Earliest Chinatown* (Victoria: Orca Book Publishers), 1991, p. 60.

46   Fan tan is a traditional Chinese gambling game, using fan tan beads, similar in concept to roulette. Due to Chinese presence since the gold rush, fan tan became a popular game along the Pacific coast of North America in the second half of the 19th century.

47   Ying-Ying Chen, "In the Colonies of Tang: Historical Archaeology of Chinese Communities in the North Cariboo District, British Columbia." Simon Fraser University, PhD dissertation, 2001, p. 320. https://www.lib.utexas.edu/etd/d/2008/cheny36960/cheny36960.pdf, *accessed March 5, 2014.*

48   Lee 1967, 88.

49   Henry Yu, "The Intermittent Rhythms of the Cantonese Pacific." In *Connecting Seas and Connected Oceans: Indian, Atlantic and Pacific Oceans and China Seas Migration from the 1830s to the 1930s*, edited by Donna R. Garbaccia and Dirk Hoerder (Leiden: Brill), 2011, pp. 393-414.

50   See Sinn 2013.

Ceramic beer bottles. German and Bavarian brewers came with the gold-rush miners and built BC's first breweries.
RBCM 989.23.223; RBCM 989.23.224; RBCM 989.23.222

Women in the Fraser and Cariboo Gold Rushes, 1858–70

Marie Elliott

||||||||||||||||||||||||||||||||||||||||||||||||

ONE COULDN'T ASK for a more fascinating cast of characters than the women who took part in the Fraser River and Cariboo gold rushes. Among them were First Nations and Metis, Chinese, German hurdy gurdy dancers, a French courtesan, an American black poet and English clergymen's wives. Although their time on stage was usually brief, their roles were crucial to the social, economic and spiritual health of the gold fields.

The rugged Coast Mountains and deep canyons of the Fraser River amazed the gold-rush newcomers in 1858, but they soon discovered that the First Peoples living here, women included, knew the landscape intimately. In fact, more than a few Hudson's Bay Company (HBC) personnel were married to local native and Metis women. Justine Allard, the wife of HBC clerk Ovid Allard at Yale, was the sister of a Cowichan confederacy chief named T'Soshia. Mary Ann Charles, the Metis daughter of HBC clerk James Birnie, had recently married William Charles, also Metis, the clerk in charge of Fort Hope. The walls of the company's forts protected these women and their children from the rowdy activities of the gold seekers, while Coast Salish women moved among the miners, earning income from transporting men and supplies in canoes, packing goods over the trails, gathering fodder for horses and mules, or selling fish and wild game.

because the river remained high into August. On the few exposed sand bars miners waited out the rainy summer by washing the accumulated tailings. At least one woman was on the river with her husband. A *Daily Alta* correspondent wrote from Hill's Bar on August 4 that a man named Newman was making $100 a week. "His wife rocks the cradle and cooks, while he picks and shovels and does the hard work."[1] About this time Malvina and Peter Toy arrived from Cornwall with their young daughter, Mary Louise, and Peter's mining partner, James Uren. The men worked claims on Cornish Bar just south of Hope, but eventually Peter headed for the interior, leaving Uren to care for his family. James and Malvina followed the gold rush as far as

By personally visiting mining sites along the Fraser River in June and September 1858, James Douglas, governor of Vancouver Island, strived to ensure that the miners understood men and women of all races were to be treated equally under British law. Native, European, Chinese and black women could lay charges and testify in court. To support the laws and the new Gold Mining Regulations, in 1859 assistant gold commissioners with the power of magistrates were deployed to Port Douglas on Harrison Lake, to Hope, Yale, Lytton and Lillooet on the Fraser, and to the border crossings at Osoyoos and Rock Creek. As the miners surged inland, more commissioners were assigned to Williams Lake, Kamloops, Williams Creek and the Kootenays. Thus, the arrival of gold-rush women was cushioned by the presence of native women and British law administered by magistrates; there would be help for chores, childbirth and legal problems. Women would survive the gold rushes as well as men.

Placer mining on the lower Fraser River between Hope and Yale was difficult in 1858

Clinton, where they managed a hotel and operated a pack train under Malvina's name. The couple married in 1882, after Peter Toy was presumed drowned.[2]

Mary Louisa Pringle, granddaughter of a Scottish Highland border chief, was up to the challenge of bringing her family to a gold-rush village. She wrote to her father-in-law, "I feel convinced it is His will that I should go there." Pringle's husband, Reverend Alexander St David Francis Pringle, had been stationed at Fort Hope, and she had received £200 from the Society for the Propagation of the Gospel on the condition that she would remain in British Columbia with him for the next four years. She arrived at Fort Hope with children Fanny, Beatrice and baby Henrietta in the fall of 1860.[3]

When spring arrived, Mary Louisa planted a large garden with berry bushes, vegetables and

Mary Louisa Pringle about 1865. BCA G-02417

Indian Reserve at Fort Yale, September 1862. Sarah Crease sketch; BCA D-02126

flowers, and purchased a cow and chickens to ensure that the children had "healthful food". While Rev. Pringle oversaw the building of Christ Church and visited road crews working in the Fraser Canyon, she taught Sunday School and befriended young mothers Mary Ann Charles and, at Yale, a Mrs Reeve and Annie Sanders, wife of assistant gold commissioner Edward Howard Sanders. By the time the Pringles' four-year term was up two more children had been born to the family.[4]

Gaining access to the Cariboo gold fields in 1859 was challenging and expensive. Few women used the first route to the interior, the difficult Harrison-Lillooet trail that Governor Douglas had opened in the fall of 1858. When they did, they likely slept outdoors or in tents rather than on the crowded stopping house floors. Packers soon opened out the ancient First Nations trail along the steep, rocky banks of the Fraser Canyon; however, major work on a wagon road did not commence for three more years. Governor Douglas worried that men and women would starve in the interior, but packers hauled provisions up river to Lytton at low water, using Whitehall boats, and improved the canyon trail.

Women using the dangerous Fraser Canyon trail gained confidence to deal with the challenges 200 kilometres farther north. On the hastily made, 90-kilometre pack trail from Williams Lake to Quesnel Forks, they climbed over and under burned trees and navigated around murky swamps filled with dead horses, all the while fending off swarms of mosquitoes and blackflies. Stopping houses soon sprung up, but only one at Quesnel Forks was owned by a woman, Catherine Lawless.[5] When prospectors found gold at Antler Creek during the winter of 1860–61, travellers took the 30-kilometre rough trail beyond Quesnel Forks to Keithley Creek then faced a steep 25-kilometre climb over the Snowshoe Plateau (so named

because snowshoes were necessary from November to May). As prospectors roamed further afield, discovering Grouse, Williams and Lightning creeks in late 1861, the pack trail was extended more than 14 kilometres to serve the new sites. This involved a second, steep 10-kilometre climb out of Grouse Creek and over Bald and Proserpine mountains.[6]

Due to the delay in building the Cariboo Road, almost everyone – cattle drovers, merchants, gold commissioners, lawmen (including Judge Matthew Begbie), miners and women – wanting to reach Antler and Williams creeks in 1861 and 1862, had to go by way of Keithley Creek and the Snowshoe Plateau.[7] A rough, government-sponsored trail from Quesnelmouth to Williams Creek was not opened until late July 1862, and there was no permanent

ROUTE OVER FALLEN TREES.

The hazardous pack trail to the Cariboo. BCA H-02889

Quesnel Forks, 1864. Frederick Whymper watercolour on paper; BCA PDP00112

steamer connection between Soda Creek and Quesnelmouth until the spring of 1863.

When faced with the steep ascent to the Snowshoe Plateau at Keithley Creek many gold seekers decided to return south, rather than carry equipment weighing 20 kilograms or more any farther. It was a major accomplishment to reach Antler and Williams creeks in the early years, especially for European women. Some donned men's trousers and boots to save their wardrobes. Before decent access was established, all women who made their way to the gold fields were heroines, including the First Nations women who packed in supplies, pulling sleds over the snow in winter.

Irish-born Johanna McGuire was one of the first European women in the Cariboo. Run out of San Francisco for operating a brothel, she had briefly lived at Yale where she met miner Ned Whitney. He prospected nearby when she set up a grog shop at the old site of Fort Alexandria in 1859 and spent the winter at Quesnel Forks. During the summer of 1861, six women were supposed to be at Antler Creek: packer Redheaded Davis's First Nations wife, a Mrs Bailey, Everina Rice, Margaret Cusheon, her mother and her daughter. Margaret Cusheon and her family did their best to operate a saloon and stopping house but couldn't prevent the sleeping quarters from being overrun by fleas and lice. Patrons preferred the saloon floor. When Mrs Davis became mentally ill at the end of August, the miners took up a collection to send her down to New Westminster.[8]

Sophia Cameron about 1860.
BCA D-07952

Despite the difficult access, 1862 proved a bonanza year when Billy Barker discovered the gold lead 50 feet deep, below Black Jack Canyon on Williams Creek. The first long-term business people arrived with the new wave of gold miners. A pregnant Anna Cameron, with husband Robert and sister Elizabeth Roddy, established the first hotel lower down the creek, at a site called Cameronton. Anna gave birth to the first baby on the creek in the fall. Janet Morris arrived with her husband from Fifeshire, Scotland, and Mary and William Winnard from Fort Langley. Before setting out for the interior in early June, Mary had placed their three daughters, Annie, Elizabeth and Emily, with the Sisters of St Ann in Victoria. Also present were miner John "Cariboo" Cameron and his wife Sophia, still grieving the loss of their 14-month-old daughter, Mary Isabella Alice. The child had died in February, shortly after they arrived in Victoria, and was buried in the Pioneer Cemetery.

Two thousand men worked in the vicinity of Williams Creek during the summer of 1862, and about a hundred remained on their claims through the winter. It was inevitable that mountain fever (typhoid) would make its appearance in a narrow mountain valley lacking proper waste disposal. Sophia Cameron became a victim despite the care of a Canadian medical doctor, John Wilkinson. Before dying she begged her husband to take her home to Cornwall in Canada West (Ontario). Cameron vowed to keep his promise, but Sophia's death coincided with the discovery of an immense amount of gold in his claim. His only choice was to place her body in a metal-lined coffin and carry on mining until severe weather stopped work.

In late January 1863 Cameron placed Sophia's coffin on a sleigh, topped it with provisions, a two-gallon keg of rum, and a 50-pound (23-kg) bag of gold, and set off in the snow over Bald Mountain to Keithley Creek and Quesnel Forks. When he arrived at the Forks Johanna begged him not to continue because smallpox was raging in the Cariboo. But he carried on with mining partner Robert Stevenson, reaching Victoria in late February. He had Sophia's coffin buried next to his daughter's grave, then returned to Williams Creek, mined all summer, and brought out another large amount of gold in the fall. The coffins were disinterred, taken by way of the Panama, and buried at Cornwall. When rumours spread that someone else might be in Sophia's coffin, Cameron had it disinterred and opened to satisfy her family. Then for the third time she was finally laid to rest.

The year 1863 was one of the best of the gold rush, with miners recovering about $3,913,000 worth of gold (a small portion was from the

Kootenays).⁹ The Cariboo Road ended at Soda Creek, where the steamer *Enterprise* took passengers up the Fraser River to Quesnelmouth, and in September a major link, the Alexandra Bridge spanning the Fraser near Yale, was opened for vehicle traffic. Women arrived in greater numbers. They were needed as boarding-house keepers, laundresses, saloon keepers and restaurant managers. The Cusheons moved from Antler Creek and opened a hotel in Cameronton. In June, black barber Wellington Delaney Moses arrived with Rebecca Gibbs. The only woman of colour among 20 white women, she may have remained for the summer helping with laundry. Following the death of her husband in Victoria, she returned to Barkerville to work as a nurse and laundress. Her poetry was published in the *Cariboo Sentinel* and the African-American newspaper, *The Elevator*. She also bought a claim in the all-black Reid mining company. Another black woman, Ann

Bodice of a silk taffeta dress that belonged to a woman in the Pemberton family in about 1860. The plaid pattern, wide sleeves and fringe decoration are typical of the fashion at that time. The white cotton undersleeves and collar were removable for washing. A distinctive bell-shaped skirt (not shown here) was worn with petticoats over a wire-hoop crinoline (see page 108). RBCM 975.110.7A-B

Hickman, arrived in 1868 and opened a restaurant at Barkerville. Both women lost their residences in the 1868 fire but Gibbs rebuilt and Hickman relocated to Richfield.

By mid December 600 men, 42 women and 7 children remained to spend the winter at Williams Creek; five companies were still working. The completion of the road to Soda Creek and the introduction of a steamboat service from there to Quesnelmouth generated more settlement and business at each terminus. Pioneer settlers Peter Dunlevy and James Sellars (Sellers) of Beaver Valley, both with First Nations wives and children, moved closer to the Cariboo Road. Dunlevy built the Exchange hotel at Soda Creek and Sellars erected a house at Mud (McLeese) Lake.

The Chilcotin Uprising dominated 1864. It is very much part of gold-rush history because construction of a proposed road across Tsilhqot'in territory to the gold fields caused the unrest. The 19 fatalities included one Tsilhqot'in woman, Klymt-edza. At Fort Alexandria in June, Adelaide Manson, Metis wife of the HBC clerk William Manson (and granddaughter of Peter Skene Ogden), coped first with the influx of 60 miners and guides recruited by gold commissioner William George Cox at Barkerville to help quell the uprising. Then in August the new Governor of British Columbia, Frederick Seymour, arrived by way of the Chilcotin to visit Quesnelmouth and the Williams Creek mines. After the court trial at Quesnelmouth, before Judge Begbie, Cox suggested that the Mansons care for two Tsilhqot'in women who had testified, Il-se-dart-nell and Nancie, until hostilities settled down. For her actions during the uprising and subsequent assistance to new settlers in the eastern Chilcotin, Nancie Swanson is revered as a heroine.¹⁰

Adelaide Manson about 1865.
John Savannah photograph.
BCA I-68892

tion death could have been caused easily by a fall. When Whitney appeared with his lawyer in court on December 12, charged with assault, he insisted that he was not guilty, and in view of the coroner's report the judge discharged him. Johanna McGuire was buried in the Pioneer Cemetery, with Anglican Bishop Edward Cridge conducting the service. Whitney is supposed to have returned to California.[12]

Sophie Roulliard, aged 25, a native of Calais, France, was found dead in her cabin at Barkerville, on May 28, 1868. The inquest decided that she had died of natural causes "accelerated by the use of strong drink", but evidence suggested otherwise. Pierre Gautier stated that Roulliard had loaned Caesar Cassiar $400, but when she tried to recover the money, eight to ten days prior to her death, "he said he did not owe her anything and struck her a blow on the stomach." Dr Thomas Bell testified that she had complained of her stomach being on fire since March, but he found no marks on her body except several small bruises.[13]

The miners on the creeks were invariably generous when a collection was taken to help someone in need. Mary Winnard had died suddenly in February 1865, from a possible heart attack, and on June 7 a charitable event was held for the benefit of her children, in order to send them back to St Ann's Academy. The Winnards had reclaimed Annie and Elizabeth from the Academy in 1864, but Emily remained there until her marriage in 1878. Mrs Charles Lowe volunteered to take the girls to Victoria, and on the way down the Cariboo Road she gathered more donations. But according to the Academy's records, the girls were never re-admitted. Mrs Lowe is supposed to have absconded with her lover David Hamburger, a former merchant on Williams Creek, and whatever became of Annie and Elizabeth Winnard remains an unsolved mystery. Vital Statistics records at the BC Archives contain no information about them.[14]

During the first decade on Williams Creek, excess alcohol consumption contributed to the violent deaths of Everina Rice, Johanna McGuire and Sophie Roulliard.[11] Rice, known as Scotch Lassie, died at her cabin within sight of the Richfield Court House, and on September 19, 1864, Begbie heard a charge of murder laid against a Swiss miner, John Baumgartner. Dr Walter Black testified that Rice was found lying on her bed covered with a 76-pound (34.5-kg) mattress that required two men to lift it off her body. He believed that more than one man was involved in her death. After the jury declared Baumgartner not guilty, the colonial government posted a reward of £100 but the murderer was never found.

Johanna McGuire was probably murdered, too. At the end of the 1864 mining season, she and Ned Whitney came down to Victoria for the winter and began drinking heavily. Following a prolonged bout, she was admitted to hospital, insensible, and died the next day. At the coroner's inquest Dr Trimble testified that in such an advanced stage of inebria-

By 1869 Williams Creek generosity was at low ebb when Reverend James Reynard, his wife, Mary, and their three children arrived to establish an Anglican Church. The family spent two miserable winters living in a small cabin at Richfield while Reynard designed and built a rustic, carpenter Gothic-style church. Since donations were sparse, he paid the wages of carpenters John Bruce and James Mann from his small salary. St Saviour's remains an outstanding architectural feature at Barkerville to this day.[15]

At this time Oblate priests from Williams Lake established St Patrick's church in a donated cabin at Richfield. Michele Lallier boarded the priests and actively canvassed for donations to support the church.

Parasol used by gold-rush entrepreneur Jane Wilcox from 1858 to 1862. After spending time in the California and Australian gold fields Wilcox and her husband came to Victoria in 1858 and opened a hotel. RBCM 2003.14.1

Cariboo quartz-and-gold brooch. In 1864 gold-rush journalist and booster Donald Fraser presented this brooch to his friend Amelia Douglas, the wife of former colonial governor James Douglas. RBCM 980.38.1a-b

FLORENCE WILSON

FLORENCE WILSON was one of 60 English women sponsored by the Columbia Emigration Society, who arrived on the bride ship *Tynemouth*, September 17, 1862. Most of the women remained in Victoria and soon married or found employment, but Wilson was self-reliant and quite capable of making a living on her own. She initially worked as a seamstress and salesperson of small personal furnishings, then opened her own store on Government Street. In March 1864 she sold off everything at cost and left the city.

Wilson headed to Barkerville, where she opened a small saloon that she made available for meetings. The public learned of her feistiness in February 1865 when newspapers reported she had tramped through part of the snow-choked Fraser Canyon on snowshoes. Two months later she returned to Williams Creek with 130 books that were purchased by the gold commissioner and donated to the Cariboo Literary Institute. When the September 1868 fire destroyed her saloon, she had it rebuilt next door to the Theatre and Fire Hall. She called it the Phoenix, after the mythical bird that rose from the ashes.

Wilson's major contributions to the Williams Creek community were her performances with the

The Cariboo Amateur Dramatic Association, July 1872. Wilson may be the woman dressed in white at the centre. BCA I-68892

FANNY BENDIXEN

Cariboo Amateur Dramatic Association. While living in Victoria she had sold tickets for local productions, and at Barkerville she was one of the founding members of the association. With John and Emily Bowron, James Anderson, Catherine Parker, Joshua Spencer Thompson, Dr Robert Carrall and others, she participated in numerous theatre events during the year, sometimes appearing in two different plays on the same evening. She specialized in comedies that received positive reviews.

OF ALL THE BARKERVILLE WOMEN, Fanny Bendixen is the most well known because she was a businesswoman in the area from 1865 until her death in 1899. She arrived in San Francisco in the early 1850s likely as part of the French emigration of undesirables sponsored by King Louis Napoleon Bonaparte III. These immigrants, known as "Ingots", contributed to the development of a lively French district centred around Commercial Street.

French female immigrants may have come from impoverished circumstances, but San Francisco men considered them more desirable

The St George Hotel became Driard House after the Bendixens left Victoria. Richard or Hannah Maynard photograph, about 1872. BCA B-00458

than Mexican, Chinese or First Nations women. Fanny became the mistress of Judge Edward McGowan, who bought and furnished a cottage for her, located on Pike Street between Clay and Sacramento. A young journalist boarding next door to Fanny's cottage claimed that he saw her often driving in an open carriage along Montgomery Street, "by long odds the most magnificently apparelled and the most beautiful woman in that gay and dissipated metropole".

McGowan did not tolerate competition. He began harassing Fanny after she ended their relationship and found another male benefactor. The French consul intervened to prevent further harm and arranged for Fanny's departure on the next ship to France. She did not go to France but to New Orleans, where she met Louis Bendixen. When Louisiana became a Confederate state in 1861, Fanny and Louis probably decided to leave New Orleans because of the city's strategic importance in the Civil War.[16] They arrived in Victoria in July 1862 and two weeks later were married at Christ Church Cathedral.[17]

Despite the fact that a great building boom was underway and numerous hotels and boarding houses had been erected, the Bendixens decided that higher-class facilities were needed to accommodate travellers, including families. They built a handsome brick hotel designed by architect John Wright and named it the St George, to appeal to British clientele. Advertising French cooking, gas lighting, and family suites, the hotel was considered the most elegant accommodation in the city. Judge Begbie, Colonel Moody and many government officials stayed there. In 1863 famous English travellers, Dr Walter Butler Cheadle and William Wentworth Fitzwilliam, Viscount Milton, used it as their headquarters while exploring British Columbia.[18]

Fanny visited Williams Creek in the summer of 1865, where she purchased property, arranged to rent the Parlor Saloon from William Winnard for the following year, and returned to Victoria in September. When the Bendixens' marriage ended in separation and bankruptcy in 1866, Louis went to San Francisco and Fanny to Barkerville.[19] She operated a saloon most of the years from 1866 until her death in 1899 and knew some of the French women living in the area: Michele Lallier, Julia Picot, Josephine DeVille and Marie Laurent. She quickly rebuilt after the fire of 1868 and moved to Lightning Creek for a few years to take advantage of a small mining boom. Like many of the local businesswomen, she used magistrate's court to recover debts and held interests in several mines, one being the French Company. After moving back to Barkerville in her latter years, she kept jars of candy on the counter for the school children. When she died in 1899 they sang in the choir for her funeral at St Saviour's Church. Fanny is buried in an unmarked grave in the Cameronton Cemetery.

In her will, Fanny left her earrings to Elizabeth Kelly, who had arrived in Barkerville in 1866, as the young bride of Andrew Kelly, a baker, miner and hotel owner. Besides caring for her large family,

Elizabeth and Andrew Kelly about 1900. BCA F-03014

Elizabeth nursed many of the women over the years, including Fanny and Janet Allen (Morris). Janet died of a broken neck when her horse and buggy went over the bank at Black Jack Canyon in September 1870.

HURDY GURDY GIRLS

DESPITE SIGNS that gold production was declining, 1865 was livelier than usual because the hurdy gurdy girls arrived.[20] German entrepreneurs procured the girls from poor families, with promises that they would return home with large amounts of money. They were indentured for two or three years, paid 300 guilders ($240) a year and provided with board and clothing by the manager.

The import of dancing girls from Europe was a severe test of Victorian propriety, even in a frontier city like San Francisco, their port of entry and home base for activities. In August 1859, 400 German residents of San Francisco invited fellow citizens to meet at the Turn Verein hall: "To take measures to put a stop to the employment of German girls for the dance cellars and as street musicians in the city – a custom at once immoral, degrading and shameful. It

is to be hoped that the good object of the originators of the meeting will succeed and that this stigma on the German name will be wiped out."[21]

The California state legislature took note of the complaints in 1860, enacting Bill 115 that prohibited girls under age 17 from dancing and playing music on the streets. The penalty for the girls and their managers was imprisonment. But the new law did not prevent hurdy bosses from taking the girls north to Barkerville and to other mining towns in Idaho and Montana Territories. Carefully supervised, the girls were not prostitutes.

For lonely prospectors pining for female companionship, the hurdies provided a few minutes of pleasure after the backbreaking work of mining. But daily existence was difficult for them and for other Cariboo women too. Charles Gentile's iconographic 1865 photograph of four neatly dressed, hoop-skirted hurdies posed in front of their Barkerville cabin provides a unique window into the lives of working women during the gold rush. Water barrels on the porch and stacked wood on the road emphasize that basic needs of heat and water were obtained by physical labour. And depending on the strength of the fabric in the women's voluminous dresses and petticoats, their uniforms needed frequent washing, ironing and mending after roughhouse dance sessions with the miners. A dance lasted five minutes. One of the performance descriptions claims that the women were hoisted in the air and swung like bells.

A few of the 1867 hurdies remained over the winter, and by March 1868 they were not making expenses. More girls returned at the beginning of May to Barry and Adler's saloon, where their summer stay ended in disaster. According to Frederick Dally, a photographer boarding nearby at the Hotel de France, the great Barkerville fire of September 16, 1868, began when a miner attempted to kiss a hurdy while she was ironing in the saloon's kitchen. The jarred stovepipe sent sparks into the

Top: Jeanette Houser, Barkerville, about 1920. BCA G-09575

Bottom: Elizabeth and Edward Dougherty, wedding photograph, 1871. BCA G-06778

canvas ceiling, and within a few hours most of the buildings had burned to the ground. The fire did not extend to Cameronton and Richfield.[22]

Hurdies were still being imported to the Cariboo in 1869, four years after they first arrived, likely as a desperate measure to capture what little gold was still in circulation. Born into large, Lutheran families, the young women were adaptable, domesticated, fun-loving, hard-working, strong and healthy. They made perfect wives for the miners who wanted a helpmate to run a hotel or a farm and stopping house on the Cariboo Road.

Two hurdies with the same surname, Rosa and Elizabeth Haub, came from two of the largest family groups in Nieder-Weisel, the Haubs and Hausers.[23] With cessation of wars and pestilence, the Hessen village had doubled in size in the previous century and was now poor and overcrowded. Gold rushes in California, Australia and British Columbia offered a chance for a brighter future.[24] Elizabeth Haub married Jacob Mundorf at Richfield, and their first child was born one month before the 1868 fire. They operated a roadhouse at 124 Mile Post on the Cariboo Road, north of Ashcroft, and had four more children. At age 26, Rosa Haub married Ephraim Langell (or Langille), a miner from River John, Nova Scotia, at Victoria, on October 3, 1874. They settled at East Sound, Orcas Island, and raised a family of 14 children.

After the Barkerville fire, 19-year-old hurdy Jeanette Ceis returned home to Langheim, Germany, and several years later brought her sister, Margaret, to San Francisco. Margaret married Charlie House and Jeanette married John Houser. They all came to Barkerville where the Houses opened a hotel and the Housers opened a saloon at Stout's Gulch. Both couples and some of their children spent the rest of their lives on Williams Creek.[25]

Elizabeth Ebert, from Baden, Germany, arrived in Barkerville in 1868, at the age of 17. Family history maintains that she travelled by ship with relatives to San Francisco and remembered sewing a burial shroud en route for a sailor. She is supposed to have come to the Cariboo with a family and independently found work as a hurdy gurdy girl.

Soon after Elizabeth married Edward Dougherty in 1871, they established the 126 Mile stopping house and farm at Maiden Creek, two miles from the Mundorf family. Like most of the residents in the area, they always attended the annual Clinton Ball. They loved to dance, especially the Flying Dutchman polka, but the orchestra delayed playing their favourite music until late in the evening, in order to keep their beautiful daughters available as dancing partners. After Edward died in January 1897, Elizabeth managed the farm and stopping house with her sons. Her family remembers her as strong and capable. She lived a long life and died in 1944 at age 92. The farm has remained in the Dougherty family to this day.[26]

At least a dozen more hurdies remained in British Columbia, married and had families.

CHINESE AND FIRST NATIONS WOMEN

RESIDING ON THE FRINGES of Williams Creek society, Chinese and First Nations women earned a precarious living. Few Chinese women arrived in the Cariboo until stagecoaches could reach Barkerville in 1866. Isolated and dependent on the men who brought them to the country, they endured miserable, lonely lives far from their families residing in the Pearl River Delta of southern China. However, they could appeal to the magistrate or a police constable and lay a charge against an offender for violence or theft. The *Cariboo Sentinel* carried the occasional story of a prostitute who managed to get an inebriated white miner removed from a brothel; other reports told of acid attacks and shootings.

When organized Chinese tongs came to Barkerville, they established several Chinese brothels patronized by both white and Chinese men. Opium was freely available, and a few women may have remained after they had paid off their indentures, working as cooks and laundresses. The *Cariboo Sentinel* recorded only one Chinese couple. Oon, wife of washerman Chung Kee, age 35, died on June 18, 1871, and Chung Kee died a few months later from an overdose of opium.[27]

First Nations women also did not arrive in numbers until after 1865. During the early years of the gold rush, they came from local groups to work along the route to the interior. (First Nations women from Washington and Oregon, who accompanied American packers, did not remain in the Cariboo.) Williams Creek always had a medical doctor available, but in outlying areas First Nations women were hired for midwifery and child care. Once easier access by stage and steamer became available the women arrived from Victoria as well as local areas such as Soda Creek during the summer months. They had more agency than Chinese women and found work as laundresses or in one or two saloons known as "squaw dance houses". But alcohol soon began wrecking their lives. Some women ended up in court with drunk and disorderly charges and some died. A few laid charges if they were mistreated, and their attackers were fined.

During the last two decades of his life, Judge Matthew Baillie Begbie took considerable interest in First Nations settlement problems caused by the gold rushes. One of his concerns was the future of native women and families who had been deserted by white men after mining activity declined. In 1877 the provincial government amended the Intestate Estates Act to provide allowances to "concubines and illegitimate children of $500 or 10 per cent of the total estate, whichever was larger."[28]

By the 1870s most of the miners had left, as had the women. The 1881 Canada Census recorded 702 residents for Richfield/Barkerville/Lightning Creek, including 244 Chinese men, 14 Chinese women and 24 white women.

OVERCOMING ACCESS proved a rough introduction to life in the gold fields; building a community came next. The women who accepted the challenges deserve a special place in British

Columbia's history. It has only been possible in the last decade to correct and verify their stories through the latest technology that makes available digitized directories and newspapers, especially the *British Colonist* and *Cariboo Sentinel*. Four important collections at the British Columbia Archives, Visual Records, Textural Records, Maps and Vital Statistics, and St Ann's Academy Archives, have also helped researchers and writers place gold rush women in a more authentic limelight, on stage where they belong. ⚒

NOTES

1   San Francisco *Daily Alta*, August 19, 1858.

2   Malvina Toy and James Uren were married on March 6, 1882. BCA, Vital Statistics registration no. 1882-09-002835.

3   Alexander David Pringle letters, BCA MS0369.

4   Ibid.

5   Catherine Lawless had formerly managed a boarding house at Fort Langley and the Mansion boarding house at New Westminster.

6   Friends of Barkerville, *1861 Goldrush Pack Trail* Map (Quesnel: Friends of Barkerville), 2000.

7   Several alternative routes were opened but lacked adequate pasture for livestock and were soon abandoned.

8   *British Colonist*, September 18, 1861, p. 3.

9   Report of the Minister of Mines, *Sessional Papers,* 1899, p. 551.

10 Colonial Correspondence, Cox to colonial secretary, October 8, 1864, BCA GR 1372, F380/1; Great Unsolved Mysteries in Canadian History.com, "Klatsassin and the Chilcotin War", website, accessed November 28, 2014.

11 Matthew Baillie Begbie court notes, October, 1864, pp. 177-87, BCA.

12 *British Colonist*, December 7, 1864, p. 3.

13 Colonial Correspondence, Inquisition for Sophie Roulliard, May 28, 1868. BCA GR 1372, F973/10.

14 Carey Pallister, Sisters of St Ann Archives, Victoria, e-mail, April 22, 2014.

15 Joan Weir, *Catalysts and Watchdogs, B.C.'s Men of God 1836–1871* (Victoria: Sono Nis Press), 1995, pp. 59-63.

16 Wikipedia, "New Orleans in the American Civil War", website accessed February 2, 2015.

17 Research on Fanny Bendixen was greatly assisted by Sherri Robinson and Chris Hanna, Alpha Research, Victoria, and by Dr Sylvia Van Kirk, who generously shared her extensive collection of Fraser and Cariboo gold rush material. See also her essay, "Fanny Bendixen" for *Dictionary of Canadian Biography,* vol. 12 (website).

18 W.B. Cheadle, *Cheadle's Journal* (Ottawa: Graphic Publishing), 1931, p. 265.

19 Sosthenes Driard purchased the St George and added two floors to make 100 bedrooms. Renamed the Driard Hotel, it retained its status as the finest hotel in Victoria into the 1900s.

20 During earlier decades in Europe, young girls called *fliegenwedel-hindlers* had been recruited in the German state of Hessen by itinerant flywhisk and broom sellers as a means to attract customers. The girls danced in front of the stalls to the music of a violin or a portable hand-cranked hurdy organ.

21 *Sacramento Daily Union*, August 15, 1859.

22 Frederick Dally Papers, 1862–83. BCA MS2443.

23 "A Nieder-Weisel Story", website accessed November 27, 2014.

24 In 1852 Johannes Hauser and Katherine Haub were among the first villagers to emigrate to the Colony of Victoria, Australia, and within a few years 300 people from Nieder-Weisel had joined them. "A Nieder-Weisel Story", website accessed November 27, 2014.

25 Louis Lebourdais Collection MS0676. Also from Hessen, Georgiana Natchingall arrived in Barkerville in 1872, at the age of 18. She married hardworking miner and carpenter Joseph St Laurent, a native of Quebec, on September 5, 1874, and lived at Quesnelmouth.

26 Jeanne David, great granddaughter of Elizabeth Ebert, provided the family history.

27 *Cariboo Sentinel*, June 24, 1871; Ying-ying Chen, "In the Colonies of Tang: Historical Archaeology of Chinese Communities in the North Cariboo District, British Columbia, 1860–1940", PhD thesis, Simon Fraser University, 2001.

28 David R. Williams, *The Man for a New Country* (Sidney, BC: Gray's Publishing), 1977, p. 107.

Conflict in the New El Dorado

The Fraser River War

Daniel Marshall

||||||||||||||||||||||||||||||||||||||||||||||||||||||

DURING THE FRASER RIVER GOLD RUSH the indigenous lands in southern British Columbia were invaded by large companies of foreign gold seekers that had effectively triggered wars with First Nations in Washington and Oregon, and by extension the Fraser River War of 1858.[1] In contrast, native-newcomer interaction in the fur trade was comparatively peaceful and, therefore, had not prepared First Nations for full-fledged war. Mining, the single greatest disruptor of native lands in the American West, created a frontier defined and segregated by race, a frontier that did not recognize the British-American border and which effectively shaped the Fraser River landscape in its own image.[2] It was this sudden invasion that broke the back of First Nations' control over access and use of their territories and resources, and it shaped this aboriginal landscape into a series of foreign, ethnically-defined mining enclaves and precipitated the formation of First Nations reserves even before the British proclaimed the Colony of British Columbia in the fall of 1858.[3]

Imagine for a moment that you and your family are suddenly invaded by thousands of strangers – in this instance, foreign gold seekers, many of whom believe vehemently that "A Good Indian is a Dead Indian!" – who claim the land your indigenous ancestors have known for millennia. California mining culture, in transcending the 49th parallel, ultimately appropriated "Indian country". During the transformative year of 1858, many Americans hoped that the US Boundary Commission would establish the gold fields south of the border, but until such time as the boundary was physically

determined, many American gold seekers
organized and operated in the Fraser gold fields
to the point of asserting near-sovereign control.
This foreign presence also brought to the "New
El Dorado" the kind of notorious genocidal
practices for which California was so well known.

By direct land communication with the Fraser
and Thompson rivers, large numbers of gold seekers
collected into even larger groupings for mutual protection and the armed incursion of eastern Washington and British Columbia. If the groups started
out consisting of only of five or ten miners, the men
simply waited at points along the Hudson's Bay
Company (HBC) brigade trail for more gold seekers
to augment their forces – perhaps 50, 100 or even
exceeding 250.[4] Miners organized themselves in the
same manner that settler-soldier armies had formed
in Washington and Oregon in the Indian Wars prior
to 1858. With the defeat of Lieutenant Colonel E.J.
Steptoe and the US Army by 1200 of the Spokane,
Palouse, Coeur d'Alene, Yakima, and other First
Nations during May 1858, much of eastern Washington was considered off-limits to civilians.[5] Companies of gold seekers, however, held a very different
view. Although Steptoe "flying before the Indians"
demanded that miners "not go beyond where the
Government could give them protection. This they
would not consent to do, but pushed on."[6] Perhaps
the best known of these companies were those that
mustered at Oregon City under the immediate
command of David McLoughlin.[7] Richard Willoughby, an "Indian-fighter" from Missouri and later
a "Texas Cowboy" in the punitive raids into Mexico,
recalled the military-style precision with which the
McLoughlin Party proceeded to Fraser River:

The miners fully realized the dangerous
undertaking it was to force their passage through
numerous warlike Indians and therefore remained
for some time at Walla Walla [Washington] await-
ing the arrival of other parties so as to organize
a larger body for mutual protection.... Probably
there was never a party on the Pacific Coast better
qualified for Indian warfare than this, the majority of the men having had long years of experience in this venturesome life and who had served
the United States Government in the war with
Mexico.[8]

Judge Robert Frost of Olympia, Washington
wrote of his membership in the McLoughlin company and the skirmishes that happened en route
to the Fraser, including the significant ambush
of their party by Chief Tenasket of the Okanagan
peoples at what was later to become known as
McLoughlin's Canyon. Frost reported: "The object
of the Indians was to get us all in the Canyon, and
had they succeeded, very few if any, would have
gotten out alive."[9] As it was, six men were killed
and the party of about 150 miners were driven back
and forced to cross the Okanagan River before
continuing north. By the time the party crossed
the 49th parallel, further skirmishes occurred, but
this largely American force finally concluded a
peace agreement at present-day Penticton.[10] John
Callbreath, a New Yorker who had sailed around
Cape Horn to San Francisco in 1849, also took this
overland route. Callbreath's company waited on
the trail to augment their numbers, elect a captain
"and organize for a hostile country". Their party
of 250 miners marched up the Columbia River,
through the Grand Coulee and ultimately into
McLoughlin's Canyon before crossing the border
towards Fort Kamloops. By this time, eastern
Washington was aflame with violence as US Army
troops sought retribution for Steptoe's defeat.
Callbreath wrote that once the company crossed
the border, "We now considered ourselves past the

most dreaded Indian country."[11] Yet other companies recorded that conflict continued on the British side of the line.

H.F. Reinhart, a young German immigrant who grew up in New York and Illinois, travelled in 1851 to California in search of gold. In 1858 he joined Major Mortimer Robertson's party of about 250 miners preparing at The Dalles, Oregon, to go north to the Fraser River. Reinhart wrote that Robertson "said if he could make up a company of 300 men with plenty of arms, ammunition, horses and mules and provisions, he would take us to Fraser River if we had to fight the Indians every day."[12] Major Robertson's prognostication was not far off the mark. Of the indigenous people, "most of my men seem eager for a fight with them," claimed Robertson, "and I am disposed to think their desire will be gratified before one week has elapsed."[13] Open hostility and general skirmishes with native peoples are recorded throughout Reinhart's extensive recounting of the trip north: "The old Californian miners and Indian-fighters were the worst,"

Reinhart lamented, as they believed "they could travel in small parties and clean out all the Indians in the land."[14]

Once inside British territory, tensions were certainly no better. At Okanagan Lake these gold seekers showed horrific force. Concealed within a gulch, they waited for members of the Okanagan Nation to arrive. "As soon as the Indians saw the whites," wrote Reinhart,

> they were so frightened that some turned back and ran towards their boat, some fell down on their knees and begged for [them] not to shoot, as they had no arms at all, and they threw up their hands and arms to show that they had nothing. But the whites all commenced to fire and shoot at them, and ran out to the lake after those getting in their canoes, and kept on shooting till the few that got in the [canoes] got out of reach of the guns and rifles.... It was a brutal affair, but the perpetrators of the outrage thought they were heroes, and were victors in some well-fought battle.[15]

George Wesley Beam, formerly captain of the Northern Rangers, Washington Territorial Volunteers, and participant in the Indian Wars of 1856, heard rumours of these conflicts and the eventual response made by some of his fellow countrymen.[16] Writing from Puget Sound Bar on the Fraser River, Beam recorded: "The Oregonians have got to Thompson River and they clear out the Indians where ever the[y] come across them."[17] And to his friend Winfield Scott Ebey, brother of the well-known customs collector, he further elaborated: "Indian report says that they kill all siwashes that they see."[18]

While overland parties effectively extended native-white violence from Washington and Oregon into British territory, maritime routes through Victoria, Port Townsend and Bellingham Bay to Fort Hope and Fort Yale expanded aggression even more directly to the Fraser itself.[19] Conflict in the New El Dorado was inevitable once gold (and the environmental consequences of placer mining) began to rival salmon fishing and processing on these same contested grounds of the Thompson and Fraser river corridors.

As overland companies reached Kamloops, not only did they receive credible, first-hand accounts of the gold fields, but also that First Nations in the Fraser Canyon were resisting white encroachment.[20] Richard Willoughby "learned from them of the Indian War on the Fraser River which had taken place at the same time as they had their troubles on the Columbia."[21] Likewise, Reinhart in reaching The Fountain near Lillooet recorded:

There had been an Indian War lower down Fraser River and the Indians had cut off the heads of many miners, "Bostons", or Americans, until … the miners just quit work and organized into companies and went out to fight and kill all the Indians they could find, and found several camps of them, and just killed everything, men, women and children, so that the Indians were at last very glad to make terms of peace and promise not to molest miners anymore.[22]

Native-newcomer conflict on both sides of the 49th parallel became almost inevitable as American newspapers elevated the military-like prowess of the Salishan peoples and warned gold seekers that battle was imminent. The San Francisco *Bulletin* warned:

Powerful tribes of Indians *own* that country and will be jealous of its despoliation. They are unlike the Diggers of California, in comparison being athletes – robust, hardy, brave and warlike, well armed, and by no means a common foe. Man to man, in more than one conflict hereafter, Americans will find them hard to whip. It is reasonable to calculate that in these battles – which will inevitably come – and by the usual casualties of an adventure to such a rugged country, death will overtake at least one out of every five persons who go there during the first twelve months.[23]

Indeed, Governor James Douglas believed that it would require "the nicest tact to avoid a disastrous Indian War".[24] By early June 1858, during the height of the rush north, the editor of the *Bulletin* advised that miners must "prepare for a war with the savages. They will have to work with a shovel in one hand and a rifle in the other."[25]

Governor Douglas had warned that the Nlaka'pamux were actively protecting their lucrative gold trade, having "taken the high-handed, though probably not unwise course, of expelling all parties of gold diggers … who had forced an entrance into their country." Douglas predicted "that serious affrays may take place between the natives and the motley adventurers who … may probably attempt to overpower the opposition of the natives by force of arms".[26]

Douglas had warned London that First Nations, particularly the Nlaka'pamux, "expressed a determination to reserve the gold for their own benefit" and that "affrays and collisions with the whites will surely follow the accession of numbers".[27] As many as one thousand well-armed

Francisco *Bulletin* offered a lengthy synopsis of reasons for such native opposition. He stated in part:

> The Indians told him that the whites were afraid of them, and they were going to kill them all in a short time. They said the "Bostons" and their steamboats had stopped the Salmon, and they were going to make friends with the Indians below at Fort Yale, and then make war with the whites....
> The Indians have evinced a growing disposition to provoke a collision with the whites.[31]

The Victoria *Gazette* concurred, and reported: "some two thousand Indians fifteen miles above Fort Yale are assembled, evidently for no friendly purpose."[32]

The deaths of two French miners at the height of foreign occupation of the Fraser River corridor was akin to a match lighting the tinder-dry lands of the river corridors and setting the canyons ablaze.[33] With non-native gold seekers numbering in the tens of thousands, punitive action was taken by companies of white miners who organized for the express purpose of making war with the indigenous peoples along the Fraser and Thompson rivers.

First Nations began to expel miners from their territories in advance of the concerted military-style campaign of gold seekers to clear the path of resistance through the Fraser River corridor. One such case was that of Edward Stout. The 49er from Eldorado County, California, had left San Francisco in 1858 with a party of 26 miners headed for the Fraser River. After prospecting at Fort Yale Bar, Emory Bar and New York Bar for about two weeks, they decided to climb the river in search of the source of the fine flour gold that was found throughout the lower Fraser. Reaching the confluence of the Nicomen and Thompson rivers (the approximate location where Governor Douglas had suggested that gold was first discovered by a Nlaka'pamux man), Stout's party set up their basecamp near Nicomen Falls. Stout recounted that a native woman approached

miners were reported waiting at The Dalles for an appropriate moment to enter into the lands of eastern Washington, bound for the Fraser River.[28] By mid August, American Brigadier General N.S. Clarke, in command of the Department of the Pacific, ordered Colonel Wright and his men to the region to counter the Native opposition.[29] As First Nations prepared to battle once more with the American military in Washington Territory, Natives along the Fraser River also began to make more concerted efforts to thwart any further entrance of white miners into their country.[30] The Nlaka'pamux, aware of the extreme events occurring against the First Nations south of the border, began to mount greater opposition to the presence of white gold seekers in protection of their land and resources. The special correspondent for the San

Revolvers (from the top): Samuel Colt Model 1851 percussion, made in London, England, from 1853 to 1856; Colt 7 shot, .22 calibre, 1871; Ely Whitney civilian Navy Model .36 calibre percussion, 1860; .32 calibre pin fire, 1850 to 1870.

their camp one morning with the alarming news that a number of white miners had been "massacred" farther down the river "and warned us to get out of the country as they were coming after us".[34] The gold seekers quickly headed back down the Thompson River towards China Bar. "We had to fight our way through and we burned every rancherie [village] and every salmon box that we could get a hold of," claimed Stout.

> They shot at us whenever they got a chance and we did the same. They did their best to cut us off and we had a very hard trip as we had to keep clear of the river as much as possible. I was shot in the arm and breast and a number of our men were killed and wounded…. I do not know just how many white men were killed during these fights, but there were thirty six at least. The first notice which came of the trouble was one morning when nine dead bodies drifted down the river past Yale. The heads were severed and the bodies horribly mutilated.[35]

Miners' militias responded with a scorched-earth policy typical of the kind of brutal campaigns waged against First Nations south of the border.[36] As Jason Allard, son of Chief Trader Ovid Allard in charge of Fort Yale at the time, put it: "Agitations were started to clean up the Indians…. The irregular troops started for vengeance, in military formation, the stars and stripes at their head."[37] As miners evacuated the Upper River country and returned to Yale for safety, the Victoria *Gazette* reported on the first in a series of armed companies that were bent on making war. Captain Charles Rouse, an old Texas Ranger, with the assistance of his volunteer soldiers, "routed the Indians [near Spuzzum], who took refuge in the mountains; they then burnt *three* of their rancheries, destroying all of their provisions…. There have been, in all, five of

their rancheries burnt; three above the Big Canon, and two below."[38] Rouse returned to Yale, just 19 kilometres below the scene of the action, "having in custody an Indian Chief [Kowpelst[39]] … and the crowd were for lynching the Indian first and inquiring what he had done afterward."[40] While white miners claimed that they had killed nine natives, including a chief, during the conflict, it was later confirmed "from the Indians themselves" that, in fact, they had massacred 36 natives, including five chiefs.[41]

Before news reached Yale of Rouse's campaign of reprisal, a mass meeting of several thousand miners was held to organize against the indigenous peoples. Captain George Wesley Beam, while at Puget Sound Bar on August 18, 1858, recorded in his diary: "Some of the white men are frightened to death. They think there [sic] day has come and they are not ready to go."[42] Just three days later Beam wrote, "At Union Bar they got five men out of the River that was shot by the Indians. They had their heads cut off."[43] As English miner Radcliffe Quine wrote of the conflict, they "declared war against the whites but we some put an end to it, but many Hundred lives lost".[44]

Retribution was immediate with non-natives immediately disarming at gunpoint the First Nations village next to Fort Yale, appropriating the weapons for their own use in the war.[45] Euro-Americans subsequently obtained, by force, all the arms and ammunition available from the HBC at forts Yale and Hope. Typical of miners' camp-style government, a meeting was called at Fort Hope on August 21, 1858, to vote on resolutions and frame an address to Governor Douglas "on the alarming character of the gathering of Indian difficulties."[46] The excitement among the miners was described as intense "and the determination fixed to exterminate the red man".[47] Their report to Douglas stated:

> Decapitated, denuded corpses of unfortunate adventurers are daily picked up on the river, while reports have reached us of the progress of retaliatory measures on the part of whites, involving indiscriminate slaughter of every age and sex…. The brief moments allotted to me will not allow of details. It has been deemed advisable by the residents of Fort Hope to apprize your Excellency of the existing state of affairs, that your Excellency may inaugurate and enforce such a series of measures as will check the further effusion of blood, and restore tranquillity and order to this territory.[48]

By late August of 1858 the whole United States Pacific Northwest and southern British Columbia were on a war footing. Brigadier General Clarke, in charge of American Pacific Slope military operations, landed additional troops for engagement with First Nations in Washington Territory, the total command reportedly amounting to upwards of 1500 men. At the urging of Isaac Stevens, former governor of Washington and territorial delegate to Congress, the US War Department transferred a regiment from Utah and made preparations for sending an additional 400 recruits from New York.[49]

A final massive battle inundated First Peoples in the Columbia Plateau region with professional soldiers and weaponry, all provoked by gold seekers bound for the Fraser River. Colonel George Wright, commanding the 9th Infantry and equipped with Howitzers, inflicted upon the tribes a "secure defeat".[50] The number of warriors killed was reported to be at least 17, including a chief, but other opinions suggested substantially greater numbers of deaths at the hands of the US Army.[51]

Peace treaties were subsequently enforced upon First Nations containing the primary directive that all white men, whether trappers, settlers or gold miners, have the right thereafter to pass unmolested through the native lands of eastern Washington to the Fraser River.[52] While the regular troops of the US Army were engaged in eastern Washington, volunteer miners' militias were also busy clearing the path of resistance along the Fraser River. Ovid Allard wrote to Douglas from Fort Yale:

> The Miners have abused the Indians in many instances particularly at what is called New York Bar by insulting their women after they had voluntarily given up their arms. I understand that the same thing has also occurred at "Quayome". From what I can learn I have reason to believe that some 15 or 20 Indians have lost there lives and three or four whites.[53]

The Victoria *Gazette* reported from Yale, "Canoes arrived from New York, Hill's and Texas Bars loaded with armed men, who mostly joined in some of the companies formed here, and served to keep alive the excitement."[54] In all, at least five companies were to ascend the river in August 1858, each with differing views on how to reopen the Upper diggings.[55] Some were for exterminating all native peoples encountered, while others offered to broker a peace settlement supported by a large demonstration of armed force. One such company was the Pike Guards commanded by Captain H.M. Snyder, regular correspondent to the San Francisco *Bulletin*.

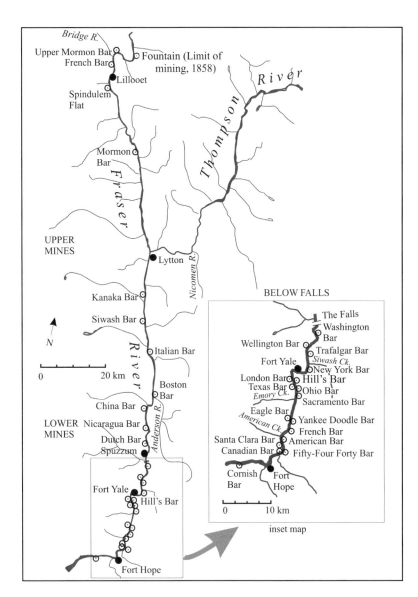

The gold diggings along the Fraser River in 1858 based on: Daniel Marshall, *"Mapping the New Eldorado: The Fraser River Gold Rush and the Appropriation of Native Space"* in *New Histories for Old* (UBC Press, 2007) Map 1.

With the newspaper's correspondent as "Commander of the Company", the *Bulletin* provided its readership with detailed field reports of Snyder's campaign.

This morning [August 18], at sunrise, three companies, armed with rifles and shot-guns, left for the upper canyons, and as far as Thompson river. One was under the command of Henry Snyder, who is well known in San Francisco. They carried a white flag, on which was inscribed, 'PIKE GUARDS'…. One party of eleven men last week went off by themselves, and succeeded in instilling a wholesome dread in the minds of the Indians…. This morning [August 19], news arrived that some more Indians had been shot, above the rancheria [Spuzzum], by the men who went up from here.[56]

During the mass meeting in Yale in August, preparations were made for the ultimate contest over the land and resources of the Fraser and Thompson rivers. In a lengthy letter to Governor Douglas, Captain Snyder told of his ten-day military-style campaign that concluded a number of treaties of peace with native chiefs from Yale to present-day Lytton. On August 16, 1858,

A company was formed to proceed at once up the river. And by a unanimous vote I was elected their Captain.... When I stated the object I had in view, and the manner in which I intended to proceed, which was to take an interpreter and make peace with the Indians by peaceable means if we could, and by force if we must, on those terms I would consent to be their commander and on no others. On taking the vote an unanimous consent was given.[57]

The main object, of course, was merely to clear the path of resistance so that white miners could continue extracting gold. Of the other companies encountered along the way though, one known as the "Whatcom Guards" called for a campaign of wholesale extermination. Snyder related to Douglas:

They wished to proceed and kill every man, woman & child they saw that had Indian blood in them. To such an arrangement I could not consent to. My heart revolted at the idea of killing a helpless woman, or an innocent child was too horrible to think of. They requested me to state my views to the crowd which consisted of six to seven hundred. I consented to do so and after I was through, and on taking the vote, I found that they were almost unanimous in supporting my course.[58]

Snyder's interpreter was HBC Trader William Yates, who accompanied the Pike Guards as far as Chapman's Bar near present-day Alexandra Bridge. Allard informed Douglas, "a party of armed men requested me to send Yates with them. I thought it would be as well for him to go with them & try to stop as many murder[s] and robbery by this said party as possible."[59] Yates noted that about 150 men accompanied them "with a white flag to give to each of the Indian Chiefs along the river, as a guarantee not to bother the whites in any shape or form".[60] Yet Yates's account noted the continued determination of the Whatcom Guards to make war. In Yates's words:

Cap[tain] Snyder learned then that an opposition party had gone by the old trail [Douglas Portage]

over the mountain and they were going to go to the lodges to kill the Indians and wipe them out, as they went through. He then rushed me ahead of the parties with 25 men to the Indian village [Spuzzum] where Captain Graham was with a party of about 50. They were going to attack the Indians. We told Captain Graham that we were sent from Captain Sneider to tell him that there was to be no attack made on the Indians. We told him to hold on until Captain Sneider and his men came up and then talk to him. He said that he would but that he was going through to wipe the Indians out if he could. The head of our party told him that he was not doing the right thing – that he had better wait until Captain Sneider came up and that they would then have an understanding about the matter. Before they got through talking Captain Sneider had come up. It was nearly dusk then. Cap[tain] Sneider got Captain Graham calmed down and told him to wait and not to be so rash as he was endangering the lives of white men by doing so. They stacked their arms there and lay down for the night.[61]

Apparently, the next morning, captains Graham and Snyder further agreed that the Whatcom Guards would remain behind and continue forth only in the event that Snyder's companies ran into trouble.

Snyder then began his original peace plan. Little did he realize at the time that while the Pike Guards made their way, Graham and his men were surreptitiously crossing Spuzzum Creek, near its confluence with the Fraser, and proceeding up the opposite side of the canyon. Snyder was alarmed to see that Graham's party had broken their promise and were advancing further up the river. Though Snyder called to them to halt, the war party paid no heed and continued to advance. Yates was again pressed into service to chase after the Whatcom Guards.[62] Snyder attempted to reason with Graham once more and "againe solicited him to joine us, but he would not". As a last resort, Snyder threatened that if Graham persisted in his plan of extermination, Snyder and the Pike Guards would head back to Yale. Graham finally did agree, once again, to allow Snyder the opportunity of brokering a peace settlement with native peoples: "And if I could make peace with the Indians & send a white flag through the canyon, that he would return to this place [Fort Yale] on those conditions and understanding."[63]

Snyder and companies finally continued their march up the river while Graham and the Whatcom Guards made camp opposite Chapman's Bar. During the course of the night, apparently pandemonium erupted among Graham's volunteer troops. Yates recalled the frantic scene. "Some of Captain Graham's men rushed right through where our men were lying," wrote Yates, "and some of them were around us and said that the Indians had been shooting at them ... we found two dead bodies in the morning."[64] Though Yates did not realize it at the time, both Captain Graham and his First Lieutenant Shaw were the ones shot dead.

After Snyder had climbed the canyon to the next native settlement, another treaty of peace was established with three chiefs and symbolic white flags issued. Snyder had promised to send a white flag to Graham, too, if the Yale-endorsed peace plan was succeeding, but the intransigent Graham upon seeing the peace flag ordered his men to "throw it away, which was done". Snyder reported, "Grayham was shot through the back at the first [fire] and died some two hours afterwards. He thinks that the Indians had watched him, if it was Indians, and had scene the treatment he gave the white flag. His firs[t] Lieutenant was also killed in the first firing. Had he done as he promised to do he would now be alive."[65] Clearly, the leadership of the Whatcom Guards had been eliminated.

As Snyder continued his campaign up the river, he achieved further peace agreements with the assistance of chiefs who accompanied him on his mission. By August 21, 1858, Snyder confirmed peace with four more chiefs before coming within 11 kilometres of the Thompson River. It was here that he first met Spintlum, "the war chief of all the tribes for some distance up & down Frazer River". Snyder continued:

> Then the War Chief made a speech to the Indians that had collected together.... He is a very cool calculating man and spoke to them for at least [a] half hour.... Here I proceeded at once to hold our grand council which consisted of Eleven Chiefs and a very large number of other Indians that had gathered from above and below. We stated to them that this time we came for peace, but if we had to come againe, that we would not come by hundreds, but by thousands and drive them from the river forever.[66]

It is difficult to say, of course, whether this bravado was intended solely for Governor Douglas, or whether Snyder actually had the audacity to state it to 11 Nlaka'pamux chiefs in the very centre of their homeland. One thing is for certain, though: the Nlaka'pamux would have been well aware of the circumstances in which First Nations found themselves south of the border. If Snyder threatened the possibility of thousands more to drive them from the river forever, it certainly would not have appeared as an idle threat considering that upwards of 1500 United States Army troops were waging a full-scale assault against indigenous peoples south of the border.

Chief Spintlum certainly had much to reflect upon. Ethnographer James Teit captured the great dilemma these people faced when he recorded the different stances of individual chiefs for and against war:

> Hundreds of warriors from all parts of the upper Thompson country had assembled at Lytton with the intention of blocking the progress of the whites beyond that point [he stated], and, if possible, of driving them back down the river. The

Chief David Spintlum's memorial at Lytton. (Courtesy of the Village of Lytton.)

Okanagan had sent word, promising aid, and it was expected that the Shuswap would also render help. In fact the Bonaparte, Savona, and Kamloops bands had indicated their desire to assist if war was declared. For a number of days there was much excitement at Lytton, and many fiery speeches were made. CuxcuxesqEt, the Lytton war-chief, a large, active man of great courage, talked incessantly for war. He put on his headdress of eagle feathers, and, painted, decked and armed for battle, advised the people to drive out the whites. At the end of his speeches he would dance as in a war dance, or imitate the grisly bear, his chief guardian spirit. Cunamitsa, the Spences Bridge chief, and several other leading men, were also in favour of war. CexpentlEm [Spintlum], with his great powers of oratory, talked continually for peace, and showed strongly its advantages. The people were thus divided as to

the best course to pursue, and finally most of them favoured CexpentlEm's proposals.[67]

Snyder may not have realized it, but it seems that the Nlaka'pamux had already decided for peace among themselves prior to the commander's ultimatum. More peace treaties were established at Lytton with a final total of 27 chiefs,[68] "a letter stating their proceedings" given to each along with white flags to show other possibly more hostile companies of gold seekers.[69] Snyder asked of the white mining population "circumspection and forbearance towards the Indians" and expressed "his conviction that the desire of the Indian is sincere for peace".[70] His white flags of peace were subsequently seen flying at all the First Nations villages that had been visited by the Pike Guards, and it is estimated that during the course of his campaign he had "entered into treaty" with at least 2000 natives.[71]

If you travel to Lytton today, you may find, hidden from general view, a large monument in the form of a Christian crucifix, erected in 1927 to the memory of Chief Spintlum. On its base are the following words that testify to the extraordinary role this First Nations leader played during the gold rush, words that are given greater meaning for us today when placed in their proper context of the Fraser River War: "When the White Men first discovered British Columbia the Indians were using the land and this caused bloodshed. David Spintlum did not want this loss of life and succeeded in stopping the war."[72]

In the immediate aftermath of the Fraser River War, Douglas and other government officials sailed for Fort Hope on August 30, 1858, "for the purpose of making treaties of peace with the Indians".[73] Douglas was spurred to travel specifically to Fort Hope in acknowledgement of the miners' urgent pleas with regard to large numbers of gold seekers having been killed. As James Teit recorded, "With the arrival of Governor Douglas and the making of explanations or promises on his side, most of the [Nlaka'pamux] people favoured peace; and finally, CexpentlEm [Spintlum], on behalf of his people, allowed the whites to enter his country."[74] What these promises were has been lost to history.

Writing to British Secretary of State for the Colonies Edward Bulwer-Lytton on October 12, 1858, Douglas stated that he had listened to all the complaints of the local native population at Fort Hope who were "much incensed against the miners". While there, he also received visits from other chiefs of the Nlaka'pamux besides Spintlum to whom he "communicated the wishes of Her Majesty's Government ... and gave them much useful advice for their guidance in the altered state of the country". Later, at Fort Yale, Douglas claimed he also listened to the complaints of natives who were there assembled, "and made no secret of their dislike to their white visitors". He noted to Lytton that "they had made complaints of maltreatment, and in all cases where redress was possible, it was granted without delay".[75] For all of the complaints and distress that Douglas undoubtedly heard, he chose not to record the particulars of extreme native-miner conflict in his official despatches to London.

One wonders how Secretary of State Lytton would have viewed a report in which the foreign mining population was found to have taken the law into its own hands, massacring significant numbers of natives, in the absence of any significant British colonial presence – especially considering that the influential Aborigines Protection Society had just made representations to him imploring that the genocidal actions of American miners in the California gold fields not be repeated in British Columbia.

Like First Nations, colonial authority was overwhelmed by the numbers of miners and their weaponry, and this foreign gold-seeking population had taken the law into their own hands. The Fraser River gold fields was not the only region where First Nations suffered the consequences of these gold-seeking *conquistadors*. In fact, the whole transboundary region of southern British Columbia and northern Washington Territory was affected. The Fraser River War of 1858, like the American Indian War in the Pacific Northwest, was a devastating contest that dispossessed First Nations of much of their traditional lands, with some further evidence to suggest an extended effect on First Nations throughout British Columbia and Washington. That little has been written about this episode speaks in part to its absence from official government records, the itinerary of the players (many of whom returned to their countries of origin), and the widespread dispersal of archival accounts that today survive in various repositories in the United Kingdom, British Columbia, Washington, Oregon, California and beyond. ✕

NOTES

1   This essay is an abbreviated version of an earlier published work. For a substantially fuller account of the Fraser River War see Daniel Marshall, "No Parallel: American Settler-Soldiers at War with the Nlaka'pamux of the Canadian West" in *Parallel Destinies: Canadian-American Relations West of the Rockies,* edited by John Findlay and Ken Coates (Seattle: University of Washington Press, 2002), pp. 31–79.

2   See Patricia Nelson Limerick, *The Legacy of Conquest: The Unbroken Past of the American West* (New York & London: W.W. Norton, 1987), pp. 99–107.

3   British Columbia was proclaimed a Crown Colony on November 19, 1858, at Fort Langley, BC.

4   Some more romanticized, jingoistic accounts inflate their numbers to as many as 800 miners forming a single armed

company. William Shannon, "Richard G. Willoughby" unpublished manuscript, BC Archives.

5   For an accounting of these battles by the commanding general of the US Army, see Thomas W. Prosch, "The Indian War of 1858", *Washington Historical Quarterly* (Oct. 1907 to July 1908) and T.C. Elliot, "Steptoe Butte and Steptoe Battle-field" *WHQ* 18 (1927).

6   Shannon, "Richard Willoughby," p. 11.

7   David McLoughlin was the son of Dr John McLoughlin, governor of the HBC west of the Rockies and considered the "Father of Oregon".

8   Shannon, "Willoughby," pp. 11–12.

9   Robert Frost to George H. Hines, Olympia, Washington, February 28, 1907. Reminiscences. OHS Library. See also, Robert Frost, "Fraser River Gold Rush Adventures." *WHQ* 22:3, pp. 203–09.

10 Shannon, "Willoughby," p. 13.

11 John Callbreath letter to his mother from Bridge River, BC, January 21, 1859. Bancroft Library, 79/93c, box 1.

12 Doyce B. Nunis, Jr, ed. *The Golden Frontier: The recollections of Herman Francis Reinhart, 1851-1869* (Austin: University of Texas Press, 1962), see chapter VI entitled "To the Fraser and Return," p. 115.

13 "The Yakima Expedition," *The Weekly Oregonian*, August 14, 1858.

14 Reinhart, p. 120.

15 Reinhart thought that 10 or 12 natives must have been killed and a similar number wounded, "a deed Californians should ever be ashamed of, without counting the consequences". Ibid., pp. 126–27.

16 For Beam's membership in the Washington Territorial Volunteers and participation in the Indian Wars south of the border, see *The Official History of the Washington National Guard, Volume II: Washington Territorial Militia in the Indian Wars of 1855–56* (Tacoma, Washington: Office of the Adjutant General, n.d.). Washington State Archives, Olympia.

17 The Fraser River Gold Rush Diary of George Wesley Beam, August 22, 1858, in *Beam Papers*, 1858–66, vol. 1. University of Washington Library. Manuscripts & University Archives Division, Seattle, Washington. Hereafter cited as UWL Archives.

18 Beam to Ebey, August 20, 1858, Pugets Sound Bar, Fraser River. Winfield Scott *Ebey Papers,* Incoming Correspondence. UWL Archives.

19 "This flooding of the country with strangers may have a tendency to rouse the whole northern Indians to an active spirit of hostility, the consequences of which will be truly disastrous to the whites; as much blood will be spilt before an opening can be affected [sic] to the [Fraser] mines." See James Beith, Letter book (1854–67), July 10, 1858, pp. 27–29. Bancroft Library.

20 British Columbia was termed the "New Eldorado" in newspapers, private letters and in an early published work, Kinahan Cornwallis, *The New El Dorado; or British Columbia* (London: Thomas Cautley Newby, 1858).

21 Shannon, "Willoughby," p. 14.

22 Reinhart, pp. 130 and 135.

23 "Something New of the Northern Goldfields," *Bulletin*, June 18, 1858, p. 2.

24 *Papers Relative to the Affairs of British Columbia* Part I (London: 1859), p. 16.

25 "People crazy to get to the new mines should not overlook the fact that mining amid a swarm of hostile Indians, is a very different thing from mining in California." See "Take It Coolly," (editorial) *Bulletin*, June 7, 1858, p. 2.

26 Douglas to Labouchere, July 15, 1857 (no. 5), in *Correspondence Relative to the Discovery of Gold in The Fraser's River District, in British North America* (London: George Edward Eyre & William Spottiswoode, 1858), 7-8. For the role of native miners in this rush, see Daniel P. Marshall, "Rickard Revisted: Native 'Participation' in the Gold Discoveries of British Columbia," *Native Studies Review* 11:1 (1997), pp. 91–108.

27 Douglas to Labouchere, April 6, 1858 (no. 8), *Correspondence Relative to the Discovery of Gold*, p. 10.

28 "Army Movements in the North – The Hostile Indians," *Bulletin*, August 19, 1858, p. 2.

29 "Army Movements in the North," *Bulletin*, August 19, 1858, p. 3. Clark was appointed to the Department of the Pacific in 1857. William F. Strobridge, *Regulars in the Redwoods: The US Army in Northern Californian, 1852–1861* (Spokane: Arthur H. Clarke Co. 1994), p. 146.

30 "Letters from Fraser River," *Bulletin,* 24 August 1858, p. 2.

31 Ibid.

32 "Indian Difficulties," Victoria *Gazette*. Reprinted in *Bulletin*, August 24, 1858, p. 3.

33 James Douglas noted the deaths of the two Frenchmen by Nlaka'pamux men in his diary entry of July 14, 1858. Yet he was noticeably silent throughout official and non-official documents with regard to the large-scale violence that was to ensue, most likely as it would have provided evidence for limited British sovereignty and that British colonial authority was being severely undermined by a foreign

mining population. See "Diary of Gold Discovery on Fraser's River in 1858", BC Archives. Ovid Allard, the HBC trader at Fort Yale wrote to Douglas about the conflict. Allard to Douglas, August 20, 1858. Colonial Correspondence. BC Archives.

34 Unless otherwise noted, most of the information found here is in "Taken from Edward Stout at Yale, British Columbia," May 14, 1908. E/E/St71. BC Archives.

35 A more detailed version of Ned Stout's account is found in "Reminiscences by Edward Stout of Yale, BC." E/E/St71. BC Archives. Also see W.W. Walkem, *Stories of Early British Columbia* (Vancouver: *New Advertiser*, 1914).

36 The genocidal treatment by white miners of California's indigenous peoples set a precedent that was to accompany the expansion of the California mining frontier throughout the Far West and British Columbia. In particular, see chapter 5, "The Varieties of Exploitation" in James J. Rawls, *Indians of California: The Changing Image* (Norman: University of Oklahoma Press, 1984), 109-133. Also, Ch. IV, "The Federal Government and the Indians," in Richard White, *'It's Your Misfortune and None of my Own': A New History of the American West*, 85-118. Heizer, *The Destruction of the California Indians*, prev. cit.

37 Jason O. Allard, "White Miners Saved Lives of BC's First Chinese – Some Stories of Yale in the Gold Rush," Reminiscences. *Howay-Reid Collection*. Box 21:4 UBC Special Collections.

38 Letter from Capt. Snyder, "The Indian Difficulties," *Gazette*, August 24, 1858, p. 3. Note: *rancheries* or *rancherias* was a Spanish term used in California to describe native village sites.

39 Kowpelst, or "Copals" as he was referred to in press reports, was a chief of the Spuzzum peoples. See Andrea Laforet and Annie York, *Spuzzum: Fraser Canyon Histories, 1808-1939* (Vancouver: University of British Columbia Press, 1998), p. 51.

40 "From The Mines: Letter From Fort Yale," *Gazette*, August 24, 1858, p. 2.

41 *Gazette*, August 24, 1858, p. 2. Capt. Rouse's company "killed, in all, some thirty-one Indians – as reported by the Indians themselves." See "Letter from Fort Yale," *Gazette*, September 1, 1858, p. 2. Also see "Another Letter from Fort Yale," *Gazette*, September 1, 1858, where it states: "The chief says that 31 warriors and 5 chiefs have been killed; he does not know how many whites." On p. 3 of same issue, Capt. Snyder reported that Rouse had "indiscriminately killed some 31 Indians, the most of whom had always been friendly to the whites".

42 Beam Diary, August 18, 1858.

43 Beam Diary, August 21, 1858.

44 Radcliffe Quine to his brother John, March 22, 1878, Seattle. Oregon Historical Society Library.

45 Ovid Allard to Chief Trader James M. Yale, stated that the salmon trade at Fort Yale was effectively suspended and Native labourers for the transport of goods to Fort Langley were not to be found as the "Indians are so much afraid" due to warring action of white miners. At the same time, Allard also noted that some 400 miners had left the Fraser in the previous four days, presumably due to the heightened conflict. Allard to Yale, 20 August 1858. Fort Langley, Correspondence In, 1844-1870. Hudson's Bay Company Archives.

46 "Miners Meeting at Fort Hope," *Bulletin*, September 1, 1858, p. 3.

47 "Letter from Fort Hope, Fraser River: The Indian Hostilities – Proceedings of the Miners," *Bulletin*, September 2, 1858, p. 3.

48 "To His Excellency Jas. Douglas, Governor of Vancouver Island, etc.," *Bulletin*, September 2, 1858, p. 3.

49 Kent D. Richards, *Isaac I. Stevens: Young Man in a Hurry*. 1979 Reprint (Pullman: Washington State University Press, 1993), p. 332.

50 "Later from Oregon: A Victory over the Indians," *Bulletin*, September 25, 1858, p. 2.

51 Glassley, *Pacific Northwest Indian Wars*, pp. 143–50.

52 "Letter from Camp in Washington Territory," *Bulletin*, October 16, 1858, p. 2. See also, "Official Report of the Indian War in the North," *Bulletin*, October 16, 1858, p. 2.

53 Allard to Douglas, August 20, 1858, CC. BC Archives. The disarming of the Yale First Nation is confirmed by Captain George Beam: "They have taken the arms from the Indians at Fort Yale so they would not join the hostiles". See Beam to Ebey, August 20, 1858.

54 "From the Mines," *Gazette*, August 24, 1858, p. 2. One of the greatest indications of the American presence on the Fraser River is the great number of California-like gold-rush-bar place names that existed. Here is a sampling of those that reflect American nationality: Fifty-Four Forty Bar, Santa Clara Bar, American Bar, Yankee Doodle Bar, Eagle Bar, Sacramento Bar, Texas Bar, Ohio Bar, New York Bar, Washington Bar and Boston Bar.

55 Ibid.

56 "An Indian War Broken Out," September 1, 1858, p. 2, and found under "Armed Companies Proceeding up the River." The Chasseur de Vincennes was a massive French fortress and the Zouaves were well-known Papal Guards.

57 H.M. Snyder, Capt. of the Pike Guards & Commander of Company, to James Douglas, Governor of Vancouver Island, August 28, 1858. Colonial Correspondence. BC Archives. The campaign lasted from the 16th to the 26th of August and the other officers elected were John Gordon, 1st Lieutenant; P.M. Warner, 2nd Lieutenant; D. McEachern, Orderly Sargeant; and P. Gascoigne, Quartermaster.

58 Snyder to Douglas, August 28, 1858.

59 Allard to Douglas, August 20, 1858. Colonial Correspondence. BC Archives.

60 "Reminiscences of William Yates." Prev. cit.

61 "Reminiscences of William Yates." Prev. cit..

62 Yates recalled: "He sent me with a party of 25 to follow him up and ask him what he meant by not sticking to his promise. He told the head of my party to tell our captain Sneider [sic] that he was on his way to hell and he hoped that he would be following him." Ibid.

63 Snyder to Douglas, August 28, 1858. Colonial Correspondence. BC Archives.

64 "The Indians had nothing but the old fashioned Hudson's Bay guns those days." Yates Reminiscences.

65 Snyder to Douglas, August 28, 1858.

66 Ibid.

67 Teit, *Mythology of the Thompson Indians*. The Jesup North Pacific Expedition, VIII:2. American Museum of Natural History Memoir 12 (Leiden: E.J. Brill, 1912), 412. Also quoted in Laforet and York, *Spuzzum: Fraser Canyon Histories*, pp. 54–55.

68 H.M. Snyder, "Letter from Fort Yale, Fraser River," *Bulletin*, September 25, 1858, p. 2. Snyder claimed that "Spintlum – is one of the finest-looking Indians that I have ever seen. He appears to have great control and influence over the different tribes. He made two speeches to the Indians. His manner of speaking is calm and cool, though with a great deal of force."

69 Snyder to Douglas, August 28, 1858. The letter of proceedings is recorded in "Massacre of Forty-Five Miners by Indians," *Gazette,* August 25, 1858, p. 2. The "treaty" was subsequently shown to Graham of the Whatcom Guards, "The Story of the Massacre of the Forty-Three White Men Untrue," *Gazette*, August 26, 1858, p. 2.

70 "Latest News from the Fraser River: Indian Hostilities – Prospects of the Diggings," *Bulletin*, September 2, 1858, p. 3. The same article noted an additional five corpses picked up from the river about Fort Yale, swelling the number to thirteen.

71 Snyder to Douglas, August 28, 1858. "Account of Capt. Snyder's Expedition," *Gazette,* September 1, 1858, p. 3.

72 As transcribed by the author. The monument to Spintlum's memory was dedicated April 16, 1927.

73 "Later from the Northern Waters: Departure of Governor Douglas for Fraser River," *Bulletin*, September 6, 1858, p. 3. See also, Douglas to Lytton, October 12, 1858, No. 3, CO 60/1, p. 213. PRO.

74 Teit, *Mythology of the Thompson Indians*, p. 412.

75 Douglas to Lytton, October 12, 1858, No. 3, CO 60/1, p. 213. PRO.

More than 400 residents of Yale signed this petition addressed to Governor James Douglas on November 22, 1858, requesting a gold escort and post offices in their town. They hoped to protect their gold shipments to Victoria. Unfortunately, Douglas could not find funds to finance a proper gold escort until 1861, when gold started pouring out of the Cariboo gold fields.
BCA GR-1372, file 1342

Another Wooden City Among The Rocks

Historic Places of the Gold Rush in British Columbia

Jennifer Iredale

||||||||||||||||||||||||||||||||||||||||||||||||||

N PREPARING THIS ESSAY I was reminded, yet again, of how significant an impact the gold rush had in shaping British Columbia. In the last half of the 19th century, world attention turned to the west coast of North America as gold discoveries became widely known – particularly those in 1849 at Sutter's Mill in California; in 1858 on the Fraser River; in 1862 on Williams Creek in BC; and finally, the "last great" gold rush along the Klondike River in Yukon and Alaska in 1898. These discoveries prompted a worldwide migration of thousands upon thousands of people, primarily men.

At this time western North America was populated by aboriginal nations, inhabiting both permanent and seasonal settlements near reliable sources of food and raw materials. While the heritage of these aboriginal cultural landscapes is certainly part of the gold rush story, it is the dramatic impact of the gold rush itself – the settlement patterns, technology and vernacular building traditions introduced by incoming miners and settlers – that significantly altered the landscape of western North America. The cultural landscape that emerged with the gold rush in British Columbia 150 years ago shaped the province as we know it now.

California, British Columbia, Yukon and Alaska share a similar pattern of migration and settlement in the gold rush era. For example, similar vernacular architectural traditions associated with gold rush activities can be found in the California towns of Bodie and Columbia, in BC's Yale, Hat Creek Ranch, Cottonwood House and Barkerville, in Dawson City, Yukon, and Skagway, Alaska.

Wharf Street, Victoria, 1858. Richard Maynard photograph; BCA A-04656

Previous spread: Looking south on Main Street, Barkerville, about 1868. Richard Maynard photograph; BCA F-07769

Today the evidence of this built heritage is becoming increasingly rare, particularly with respect to first- and second-generation buildings. The few remaining buildings give us important insights into our gold rush heritage. Some continue to be preserved at the Provincial Heritage Properties at Barkerville Historic Town, at the Cottonwood Roadhouse site and Historic Hat Creek Ranch. Remnants of this built heritage can also be found in older towns such as Victoria, New Westminster, and Yale.

Unlike other parts of North America, British Columbia has some unique aspects to its settlement process during the gold rush due to the presence of British colonial surveyors and Royal Engineers, whose impact on our province can still be seen. These men, trained in England, worked to lay out many of the settlements and roads that were constructed in the 1860s, and designed and constructed a number of early buildings.

In addition, the landscape, as it emerged during this time, reflects the evolution of mining technology from the mid 19th century onward. Mining changed the landscape along the Fraser

River to Barkerville and north. Early placer and hand mining activity resulted in carefully stacked rock piles and placer tailings that are still evident along the shores of the Fraser River. Now, visitors driving along the Barkerville Highway will pass the remains of both historic and modern mining activity at Wingdam, followed by massive waste rock dumps, mill tailings, head frames, and industrial structures from Cariboo Gold Quartz mines and Island Mountain hard rock mines, active between the 1930s and 1960s – both centred in the company town of Wells. Before arriving at the Barkerville townsite, visitors will see evidence of 21st century small-scape, open-pit mining, followed by a huge tailings pile near the entrance to Barkerville. The landscape along Williams Creek was essentially created by the hydraulic pit mining that began in the early 1890s and went on into the early 20th century. The road from Barkerville to Richfield passes through a mining landscape dotted with abandoned historic adits, over the unseen remains of the underground placer mines that characterized the Cariboo gold rush from the 1860s through to 1900.

In the spring of 1858 the Fraser River gold rush greatly accelerated Victoria's growth. From its small, fur trade origins centred around a fort, it grew to a tent village that accommodated the arrival of 6000 men. During those six weeks in the summer of 1858, 225 buildings were constructed on the townsite, which had been laid out in 1851 by the Hudson's Bay surveyors J.D. Pemberton and B.W. Pearse. Pemberton used Wakefield's town planning theory of "systematic colonization"[1] in order to purposely shape BC's mining towns, rather than have them form in the unplanned, chaotic manner of California gold-rush towns.

While early Victoria may have followed a British town plan, it also had an American look and feel. The design and building of Victoria was influenced significantly by architects such as Wright and Sanders,[2] John Teague,[3] and others who came north, bringing with them the Italianate design palette characteristic of the California gold rush.[4] A good example is to be found on Commercial Row (now 1117 Wharf Street), with its three-storey Italianate buildings designed in the 1860s by architect/builder Richard Lewis.[5] The row is characterized by distinctive cast iron columns which were imported from San Francisco and still show the foundry mark of 1861.

A fine example of residential gold-rush-era architecture in Victoria is Carr House (207 Government Street), built in 1863 by a dry goods merchant, Richard Carr, and designed by San Francisco architects Wright and Sanders. The house was built in the picturesque Italianate style using balloon frame construction techniques and an abundance of characteristic decorative wooden elements (balcony, brackets, strong vertical

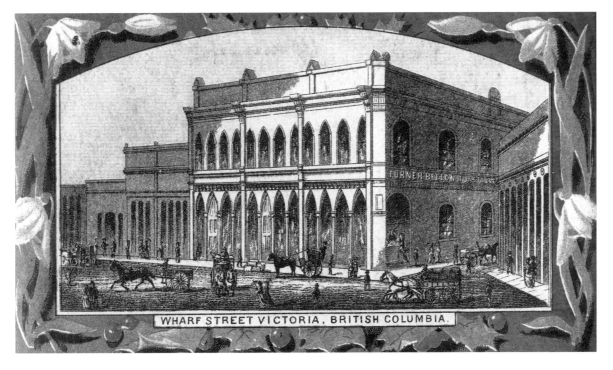

Wharf Street, Victoria, 1874. Richard Maynard photograph; BCA C-06322

window massing with rounded casings). Following the design treatise found in British and American style books, the interior was decorated with marbleized and gilded wallpapers, faux-finished slate fireplace surrounds and wood finishes on the trim and baseboards, including faux oak and bird's eye maple. Today Carr House features a restored interior appropriate to the 1870s, the era of Emily Carr's childhood. Point Ellice House (2616 Pleasant Street) is another example of the Italianate residential designs of Wright and Sanders. This house exhibits period room furnishings and artifacts from the family of Peter O'Reilly, one of BC's early gold commissioners.

Victoria has preserved some of its built heritage from the gold rush era, best seen on walking tours of Victoria's Old Town and Chinatown, both designated historic districts, and the latter also a National Historic Site.

Also of interest from this period are: the Congregation Emanu-El (1421 Blanshard Street), a one-and-a-half storey, brick, Romanesque-style synagogue, designed by Wright and Sanders and built in 1863 – now the oldest surviving synagogue in Canada; the brick Oriental Hotel from the 1880s on Yates Street, designed by John Teague and characterized by cast iron columns on the ground floor and unique angled bay windows on the upper storeys; and the stone commercial warehouses on the waterfront side of Wharf Street. Fisgard and Pandora streets feature the Victorian facades of Victoria's Chinatown National Historic Site pierced by the very narrow Fan Tan, Dragon and Theatre alleys.

In the summer of 1863 William Mark published an account of his travels to the "Cariboo Gold Diggins of British Columbia" full of warnings to prospective gold seekers and, in retrospect, full of glimpses into the emerging built environment as it arose in response to the rapid increase in population. Of Victoria he wrote:

> All round the suburbs are covered with small wooden shanties, which are rented by the labouring classes, for which they pay from four to six dollars per month, many of them are occupied by Indians and Chinamen, and they only have one room, in which they perform all their domestic duties, cooking, washing, eating, and sleeping.

There are several churches and chapels, and a very pretty cemetery in the city. The Hudson Bay Company have got several large warehouses, and other place of business, along the quay.[6]

A few days into his journey Mark arrived in Port Douglas and described it as "another wooden city among the rocks". Of Port Pemberton he wrote:

Of all the places I ever saw selected for a town, this beats all; the houses or huts were all built of wood, stuck up here and there among the rocks; there was only one decent house in the lot, which was occupied as a store and grog shop, here you could get what the called a "Square meal," for one dollar.… The log-huts were occupied by the packers and teamsters, two or three cabined together and doing all their own work.

And, of another mining camp, he said:

We finally reached Antlers Creek, tired and weary, about four o'clock in the afternoon of the 4th of July, and to a certainty, we found it a rough looking place, log huts, canvass tents, all over the place, ditches, pits, mounds of earth, flumes, trenches, and sluice boxes, pumps, &c., in fact, you hardly knew where to go.

Governor James Douglas, faced with a massive influx of men prompted by the gold rush, requested support from Britain. The British Colonial Office responded by sending the Columbia Detachment of Royal Engineers to assist with the settlement, development and security of its fledgling colony. The active presence of the Royal Engineers also ensured a strong British influence on town planning and architecture, and provided engineering expertise when it came to building roads during the gold rush.[7] Between 1858 and 1863, close to 200 Royal Engineers led by Colonel Richard Moody surveyed land, laid out towns, settled disputes, diverted rivers, constructed government and church buildings, and worked to establish the international boundary between Canada and America. They left behind traces of their ingenuity, including the gothic revival design of St John the Divine in Yale, a "corrugated iron" building preserved at the Saanich Artifacts Society site, and evidence of a unique ventilation system installed in Christ Church in Hope.

Then there is what was known at the time as the "Eighth Wonder of the World" – the Cariboo Waggon Road, still visible in the remnants of the "ruts" left by this feat of Royal engineering. The Cariboo Waggon Road was the first major road construction project in the province, and major portions of Highway 97 (and the north-south rail lines) followed this long-ago route. Settlements and roadhouses that were established during the gold rush are now villages and towns, all connected by the highways that followed. Parts of this route can still be walked: at Hat Creek Ranch, at Barkerville, in parts of the Fraser Canyon and in Manning Park. Today's traveller en route from Victoria to Barkerville can discover, if they take their time, many extraordinary places that still bear witness to the gold rush era.

Between 1858 and 1859, in an effort to stay ahead of the rush, the Royal Engineers and colonial surveyors laid out the townsites of Yale, Hope, Port Douglas and Derby (now Fort Langley). Here, entrepreneurial men had the opportunity to buy one of the new town lots and thereby seek their fortune by selling services and supplies to the miners. The Royal Engineers also laid out New Westminster, an important gold rush supply and service centre designated as the capital city for the mainland colony of British Columbia.

It was here, in New Westminster, that Captain William Irving built a fine house for himself – one that was considered the finest house in the colony at the time. Irving made his fortune during the gold rush as a river boat captain and an entrepreneur, operating steam ships that ferried miners between Victoria, New Westminster and Yale. Irving House was designed in Carpenter Gothic style (possibly from a pattern book) by Irving's good friend, artist James Syme,[8] and built by carpenter T.W. Graham. Irving House has been restored and now operates as a gold rush visitor centre.

At Hope and Yale, situated along the gold rush trail running from New Westminster up the Fraser Canyon, are gold-rush-era churches that are thought to have been designed and built by the Royal Engineers.[9] These are simple wood frame buildings with some characteristic gothic revival details evident in the porches and windows, the steeply-pitched and gabled roofs, the doorways with pointed arches, the exposed interior wooden rafters and the decorative woodwork. These buildings served as centres for Anglican missionary activities in the region and reflect the role that British social and religious institutions played in colonial British Columbia at that time.

North of Yale, beyond the Canyon and on the high plateau, are a number of gold rush roadhouses and ranches – for example, Ashcroft Manor and

Hat Creek Ranch, about 1910. BCA E-03334

108 Mile Ranch, with its monumental log barn – which helped house and supply miners on their way to the Cariboo gold fields. Another of these, Historic Hat Creek Ranch, near Cache Creek, is a fine old ranch (and now a historic site) on a stretch of the original Cariboo Waggon Road.

In 1860 Donald McLean, a former Hudson's Bay Company chief trader, saw the potential for ranching at the confluence of the Bonaparte River and Hat Creek. Soon after he settled there, Hat Creek Ranch became a hub for the Barnard's Express (BX) Stage Company, which operated freight and passenger service on the Cariboo Waggon Road from 1863 to 1913. The historic site now includes many fine examples of gold rush vernacular architecture, including the hewn-log McLean Cabin, the balloon-frame, two-storey roadhouse, and the many log barns and outbuildings, some of which were roofed with sod or hay. The historic ranch landscape shows evidence of a flood irrigation system, an innovation brought to the ranch by the Bonaparte First Nation people who worked the property.

Cottonwood House, situated east of Quesnel in the Cariboo region, was owned by the Boyd family between 1874 and 1951. It stands as a reminder of the Boyd legacy of commercial enterprise, developed to serve travellers along the Cariboo Waggon Road. This roadhouse is a handsome two-storey, hewn-log residence, assembled with finely crafted dovetail notches and built in 1864 by John Ryder and Allen Smith.[11] Preserved alongside Cottonwood House is a double barn including a horse stable with a floating floor, as well as outbuildings built with round logs later in the 19th century.

Earliest known photograph of Cottonwood House, BC, made by Charles Gentile in October 1865. BCA G-00794

A freight wagon at Cottonwood House, about 1900, showing the double barn in the background. BCA A-04026

In 1862, with the discovery of significant gold deposits in the Cariboo, a number of towns grew up along Williams Creek, including Van Winkle, Lightning, Camerontown, Barkerville and Richfield, all of which reached or exceeded a population of 5000 during the 1860s. To stabilize settlement and gain control over land development, Royal Engineers Sergeant William McColl and Lance Corporal J. Turnbull were sent to survey Richfield, Barkerville and Camerontown, where they surveyed the existing building sites and, where no buildings existed, plotted a standard 60x132-foot (18x40-metre) lot, and indicated a main street with 61 lots and 40 buildings.[12] (See the painting by Frederick Whymper on page 73.

A miner's cabin at Williams Creek, near Barkerville, about 1867. Frederick Dally photograph; BCA A-00352

Unlike more gradual forms of land settlement evolving out of a rural landscape into an urban environment, the gold rush brought about an instant increase in population and initiated a process of urbanization in the gold fields. These mining towns were shaped by geography, local materials, and accessibility to mine sites. The most common form that settlements took began with a single commercial "main" street as close to the mining creek as possible, with miners' cabins and tents located somewhat haphazardly around this street. The general availability of nearby trees for building led to an architectural vernacular centred on wood. Consequently, we can see something of the cultural heritage of these miners-turned-builders, but more obviously, we can see that the designs were influenced by the need for functional shelter. These first-generation buildings were constructed out of locally available materials and in the least complex, and fastest manner possible to simply provide amenities and accommodation for a transient population. Neither civic pride or permanence were considerations because the inhabitants did not intend to stay; miners came only to make their fortune and go home.

Log construction was common during the gold rush era because the raw materials (trees) were plentiful and the structures were quick, cheap and easy to put together. Log cabins are a characteristic form for first-generation buildings in BC, and the cabin we associate with the west was the product of builders with little knowledge of construction or design. "They were unpretentiously functional and were built with the intention of eventually being abandoned."[13] Viscount William Milton and Dr Walter Cheadle, sent out by London's Royal Geographical Society to find the best route through "gold country", describe in their journal these rough and simple log structures: "A way side house on the road to the mines is merely a rough log hut of a single room; a one end large open chimney and at the side a bar counter, behind which are shelves with rows of bottles containing the vilest of alcoholic drinks."[14]

Barkerville Historic Town has preserved a few of these "rough log huts", constructed very much as depicted in the 1867 photo of "a miner's cabin at Williams Creek" by Frederick Dally. These single-room cabins were originally built out of partially peeled logs, harvested from a variety of species, and roughly notched with a simple wedge-shaped "V" to allow stacking. Chinking between the logs was made of materials at hand – mud, gravel, straw, manure, cloth, stones and sticks. Roofs were covered with slightly overlapping shakes (wooden shingles split from bolts of wood), leaving most of the shingle surface exposed to the weather. This rough and ready approach to roof construction indicates that shelters were built quickly, and probably as temporary shelter.

As Barkerville grew from a mining camp to a boom-and-bust town, sawmills were shipped in along the 800 kilometres of the new Cariboo Waggon Road. With this development, buildings of sawn lumber began to supersede tent and log structures. Sawmills could mill the lumber for flumes, waterwheels, boardwalks and, of course, more elaborate buildings.

Left:
Barkerville's Main Street in 1868, before the fire. Frederick Dally photograph; BCA A-05969

Above:
A street in Barkerville, 1865. Charles Gentile photograph; BCA E-03940

Below:
Barkerville in September 1868, just before the fire. Frederick Dally photograph; BCA A-00355

Almost more crude and simple than the early log buildings in Barkerville are the first-generation structures built with a vertical plank construction system. These buildings are constructed with milled 1x12-inch planks set vertically and toe-nailed or spiked into top and bottom beams. The wall sheath is structural, holding the weight of the entire building, in the absence of posts, studs or other supporting structure. At Barkerville the Wylde Shoemaker Shop, the Van Volkenburg Cabin, and the Kelly Store are vertical plank construction. The Wylde Shoemaker building may pre-date the great fire of September 1868,[15] and there is a photograph by L.A. Blanc dated June 1869 showing the Kelly Store building completed.

Interestingly, on the Pacific coast of BC, prior to European settlement, First Peoples built their cedar big houses using a vertical plank walled construction system. There is evidence to indicate that this form of construction was also used to build shelters during the California gold rush and through the early years of settlement in Oregon and Washington.[16] The crudeness of vertical plank

construction suggests a quick build and temporary shelter. At the same time, it also indicates that milled lumber and nails were available, even within the small budget of a builder at that time.

The buildings constructed after the great Barkerville fire of September 16, 1868, show some construction and design details reminiscent of the origin culture of the builders as well as a greater commitment to Barkerville's emerging sense of permanence.

One fascinating structure associated with the gold rush era at Barkerville is the Chee Kung Tong building, constructed by the Hong-men society and established in Barkerville by Hung-Shen-gui and his friends in 1864.[17] Believed to have been built in the 1870s, the main building is characterized by structural, light timber framing with the vertical sheathing attached by square nails. The front façade has unique decorative signboards around the second floor doorway that distinguish this building from non-Chinese buildings of this era. The building plan – with its ceremonial hall

on the second floor and its lodgings and kitchen on the first floor – is similar to other Chee Kung Tong buildings in BC, indicating cultural antecedents,[18] and incorporating China's traditional style of load-bearing timber-frame construction.

The Barkerville Hotel, built by Johnny Knott, is the largest and most ornate building constructed after the Barkerville fire of 1868. It remains one of the finest gold-rush-era examples of a Victorian Carpenter Gothic building in BC. Built using the recently invented American balloon frame construction system, the hotel has a beautiful, cantilevered balcony extending across the front of the second floor and a small balcony extending from the window on the top floor. Both balconies have decorative woodwork detailing the balustrade, and there is a fanciful eave treatment with decorative brackets under the pitched roof gable. Archival photographs show that Knott began construction of his fine hotel right after the great fire and by 1870 the hotel was complete. Balloon frame construction and the Carpenter Gothic design idiom were both characteristic of buildings constructed during the California gold rush and the subsequent settlement of the west.

Our understanding of BC's gold-rush land-scape, and the historic places that remain, reflects an evolving historical consciousness, one that has changed dramatically since 1862. The early influx of miners and settlers viewed the landscape simply in terms of geology, an immovable mass with which they struggled to wrest gold from the ground by various means, in the hopes of "striking it rich". Their buildings were simple and rough-hewn from raw materials close at hand. Mining technology in British Columbia evolved apace with other developments – the building of roads, the growth of towns and the availability of tools, tech-nology and supplies, all of which allowed greater sophistication in construction techniques and advances in architecture. The predominant use of wood, however, continued throughout this time – informing construction techniques and design.

By the middle of the 20th century, the Cari-boo gold rush took on a new cultural meaning, as it came to be perceived as "the event" that created British Columbia. In 1958, our centennial year, the province undertook to designate a number of his-toric places significant for their gold-rush history. Barkerville re-emerged in our public awareness as

Far left: Barkerville street scene, about 1869, with the Barkerville Hotel under construction and the completed Kelly store next to it. L.A. Blanc photograph; Barkerville Archives P-0719

The Barkerville Hotel, 1894.
BCA A-03765

a historic town and tourist attraction. By this same process of designation and renewed awareness, other historic places were saved from demolition as individuals and government agencies increasingly acknowledged the importance of preserving gold-rush history on the basis of its significance to our cultural zeitgeist. This evolution has changed the way we recognize and interact with historic places; it has radically changed the meaning of these places as they have come to represent both metaphor and symbol of our (imagined) past. Today we celebrate this heritage as a touchstone to our provincial and national roots and identity.

The impact of the gold rush on western North America, and particularly on British Columbia,

cannot be understated. This gold rush gave us the beginnings of a multicultural society. It spurred the development and settlement of the land and, in 1866, it led to the creation of the province of BC. In the 1860s it was the gold rush population – in Victoria, Yale and Barkerville – that called for Confederation with Canada. The first Dominion Day celebration was held in Barkerville in 1868, an event that provided much of the impetus behind the process whereby British Columbia joined Canadian Confederation. I believe it is not unreasonable to say that Barkerville's place in history is no less important to Canada than that of Quebec City, Charlottetown or Batoche. For better or worse, the physical and cultural landscape we now take for granted would be very different if not for the gold rushes in British Columbia. ✗

NOTES

1   Richard Mackie, "Biography of Joseph Despard Pemberton." *Dictionary of Canadian Biography*, vol. 12 (University of Toronto), 2003, biographi.ca/en/bio/pemberton_joseph_despard_12E.html, accessed January 30, 2015.

2   Donald Luxton, ed., *Building the West: The Early Architecture of British Columbia* (Vancouver: Talonbooks), 2003, p. 36.

3   Ibid. p. 75.

4   See also Martin Segger and Douglas Franklin. *Exploring Victoria's Architecture* (Victoria: Sono Nis Press), 1996.

5   Luxton, p. 46.

6   William Mark, *Cariboo, A True and Correct Narrative* (Stockton, CA: W.M. Wright), 1863, p. 18; the following two quotations from p. 21 and p. 32.

7   See also Beth Hill, *Sappers: The Royal Engineers in British Columbia* (Victoria: Horsdal & Schubart), 1987.

8   Luxton, p. 54.

9   Ibid., p. 33.

10 From "The Diocese of British Columbia" in *Mission Life*, vol. 3, part 2 (London: W. Wells Gardener), p. 709.

11 See also Mike H. Will, *Cottonwood House: An Architectural Investigation, Burnaby*, report for Barkerville Historic Town, 1996.

12 Richard Thomas Wright, *Barkerville, Williams Creek, Cariboo: A Gold Rush Experience* (Williams Lake: Winter Quarters Press), 1998, p. 65.

13 John Rempel, *Building with Wood and Other Aspects of 19th Century Building in Ontario* (Toronto: University of Toronto Press), 1967, p. 34.

14 Viscount William F. Milton and Walter B. Cheadle, *The Northwest Passage by Land, Being the Narrative of an Expedition from the Atlantic to the Pacific, Undertaken with the View of Exploring a Route Across the Continent to British Columbia Through British Territory by one of the Northern Passes in the Rocky Mountains* (London: Cassell, Petter and Galpin), 1865, p. 359.

15 Wright, p. 105.

16 Bodie Historic District National Historic Landmark Nomination (unpublished), May 2008, pp. 24, 25.

17 Chen, Ying-Ying, "Building No. 84: A Symbol of the Early Chinese Freemasons at Barkerville, British Columbia", unpublished report prepared for Barkerville Historic Town, 1992, p.185.

18 Chen, "In the Colonies of Tang: Historical Archaeology of Chinese Communities in the North Cariboo District, British Columbia (1860s–1940s)", PhD diss., Simon Fraser University, 2001, p. 84.

After the Gold Rush
The History of Barkerville Historic Town

Judy Campbell

IIIIIIIIIIIIIIIIIIIIIIIIIIIIIIIIIIIIIIIIIIIIIIIIIIIIII

N THE SUMMER OF 1973, *I was working as the cook on an archaeological dig at Punchaw Lake in the Blackwater country northwest of Quesnel, BC. Our crew, being history and anthropology students, decided to take a weekend trip to see Barkerville. Following the footsteps of the gold miners before us, we stopped at Cottonwood House, one of the early roadhouses along the Cariboo Waggon[1] Road. Like Barkerville, it was being preserved as part of British Columbia's relatively new heritage conservation program.*

We parked, the only car in a lot some distance from the site, and walked toward a collection of old buildings. There seemed to be no one around. I peeked in the windows of the log house – a bedroom with an iron bed and patchwork quilt, a large kitchen with a huge double-oven wood stove, perfect for cooking for throngs of miners. I rounded the corner of the house to see clothes draped on a makeshift clothesline – a woman's chemise and pantaloons, a gingham dress with a voluminous skirt, and a set of men's "onesies". The laundry was still damp. The hair on the back of my neck tingled. No one was in sight, not even my crew mates. For a fleeting moment I thought I had slipped between the layers of time into the 1860s.

As a teenager in Ontario, I often explored abandoned farms, snooping around the detritus of forgotten lives. These relics evoked vague feelings of nostalgia, sometimes even sadness, but never this sense that I was moving in time. That morning in Cottonwood I felt that instead of experiencing history by looking backwards from today, history had moved forward to envelop me in a different reality. This experience at Cottonwood House stayed with me, and even though my experience at

*Barkerville that afternoon was very different, jostling
with crowds of tourists, I felt that Barkerville would
have that same power to pull me out of my own
reality and into the heyday of the gold rush.*

|||||||||||||||||||||||||||||||||||||||||||||||||

THE GOLD RUSHES ON THE FRASER RIVER
created and united the new colonies of British
Columbia and Vancouver Island and pushed the
Colony of British Columbia into Canadian Confederation. The new province expanded physically
and economically, and by the early 1900s lumber-
ing and agriculture overtook mining as the main
industries. Vancouver became the main population
centre and the corporate headquarters.

Meanwhile, in the mountainous backwaters of
the province, miners still worked the creeks searching for overlooked pay streaks. During the Great
Depression, "motherlodes" were discovered in Cow
Mountain and Island Mountain and the town of
Wells was built eight kilometres from Barkerville to
service the booming hard rock mines. The flavour of
the original gold rushes permeated the area and for
a while Barkerville boomed again.

By the mid 1950s Barkerville, with a population
of less than 50, had been eclipsed by its sister gold
mining town, Wells. With the construction of pulp
and paper mills and the resulting growth in the
forest industry, both centres were soon overtaken
by the towns of Prince George and Quesnel.

The significance of Barkerville had been
recognized in 1923 when the National Historic Sites
and Monuments Board designated Barkerville
a National Historic Site of Canada. In fact there
were two national designations at Barkerville. The
town itself was recognized as the centre of the
Cariboo gold rush that ultimately resulted in the
formation of the Colony of British Columbia and
later Confederation with the young Dominion of
Canada, which now stretched from Atlantic to
Pacific. The other designation was for the Cariboo
Waggon Road completed to Barkerville by the
Royal Engineers in 1865 and sometimes hailed as
the Eighth Wonder of the World.

Local residents had discussed the restoration of
Barkerville for several years. Letters were written;
projects were started. In 1952 the Barkerville branch
of the Cariboo Historical Society was formed with
assistance from Alvin Johnston. Volunteers – including such notable Barkerville personalities as Bill
Hong, Lottie Bowron, Sid and Mildred Danhauer,
Mac and Jean Grady, Eric North, the Bobiers, the
Browns, the Kellys and the Tregilluses – would soon
devote countless hours lobbying those in high places
as well as organizing on-the-ground projects to prop
up and restore the mouldering heritage town.

In 1953 Fred Ludditt formed the Barkerville
Historic and Development Company with the
intent to attract investment for the restoration of
Barkerville. Fred had been troubled for years by
the decline of Barkerville:

I wished at the time I could buy every old
building in Barkerville and preserve it.

Tourists and souvenir hunters used to load
their cars with chairs, tables, mirrors, books,
letters and photos. They seemed to have no qualms
and would find their way into any building that
was not occupied. Where we, in Barkerville, would
not have dreamed of entering a building just
because its owner had left the town, even if he had
gone years ago, they thought nothing of breaking a
window to get in, and of taking out whatever they
wished. To them this was just a ghost town.

What with one thing and another I used to look
at Barkerville and see it in the future failing, eventually falling to ruin, its history unknown and its story
untold; and so I resolved to do something about it.[2]

The Chee Kung Tong building, about 1959. The building has since been restored and in 2009 was designated a National Historic Site of Canada (Barkerville's third such designation). Barkerville Archives P0638

It was a herculean task. In 1958 it was reported that:

> Many of the buildings are very old and their foundations were in the last stages of disrepair. Some were condemned by the fire marshal and others were in such a state of collapse that they were being burned to lessen the fire hazard or being cut up for wood.[3]

Adding even more urgency was the mining company that was buying up properties downstream from Barkerville and slowly working its way toward the town with a large dragline dredge, destroying everything before it and leaving in its wake a barren wasteland of gravel tailings.

The local efforts to preserve and draw attention to Barkerville were fed by the passion of volunteers for whom Barkerville was home or held some special significance. They wanted to share it with the rest of BC and Canada, but lacking the resources to realize their dream, they lobbied the province to become involved. In fact the project was a perfect fit for the government agenda at the time. It was a period of province building, with many large scale public works such as highways and dams being completed, yet it appeared at this time that British Columbia had little sense of self-identity.[4] A project such as Barkerville would provide a historical foundation and a social and psychological framework that would help to knit the province together.

The stars aligned. The centennial of the Colony of British Columbia was coming in 1958 and the province prepared to celebrate. The newly elected MLA for Cariboo was Bill Speare, a strong supporter of the efforts to save Barkerville. Speare spoke persuasively of Barkerville in his first speech to the Legislative Assembly and presented a resolution supported by the BC Centennial Committee that set out a basic program to preserve Barkerville. This was enough for Premier W.A.C. Bennett to authorize the program as part of the centennial celebrations. Government had no previous experience with heritage, so the program was given to the Parks Branch of the Department of Recreation and Conservation with noted naturalist and outdoorsman Chester P. (Ches) Lyons in charge. Fred Ludditt was hired to coordinate the first season's work at Barkerville.

Having a vision for a historic site was one thing; implementing it was another. Barkerville was not quite a ghost town. There were 25 residents or absentee landowners and numerous overlapping placer and mineral claims. An initial start was made with a number of lots that had reverted to the Crown at the south end of town. Authenticity was the primary concern, and it was soon realized that "an authentic and complete program was dependent on the eventual purchase of all land and holdings within the old townsite".[5] The provision of modern services, such as space for parking, a picnic area, campgrounds and a museum, would require additional land surrounding the site.

Landowners and residents were offered fair market value for properties – the value before

Leather water bucket used by the Barkerville Fire Department in the early 1860s. A devastating fire in 1868 destroyed all but one building in the lower section of town; miraculously no one died in the fire. The residents rebuilt the town quickly and Barkerville enjoyed several more decades of prosperity. RBCM 965.1063.1

Parks Branch staff and the originators of the restoration, resulting in frayed tempers and, in many cases, permanent hostility. However, as Ludditt himself said, there was "much to offset these disappointments and create for the visitor a feeling of having stepped behind the curtain of time into surroundings and sights of more than a century ago".[7]

The next few years would see the restoration proceeding at full tilt. Surrounding lands were acquired for services, and building restorations were underway. Missing buildings were accurately reconstructed after careful examination of the photo record. A new museum was planned to open in 1962 along with live theatre and a historic re-enactment of Judge Matthew Baillie Begbie. Articles on Barkerville appeared in travel magazines and visitor numbers expanded rapidly. The dream was coming to life!

it became known that government wanted to purchase the properties. Residents could continue to live on their property without paying rent or taxes until they chose to move away. For some who occupied buildings that were not wanted for the restoration, there was the option to have their home moved to New Barkerville, a small hamlet near the cemetery and outside park boundaries. Property in Barkerville had been worth very little, and many were happy they could sell their properties at all. But some, either sensing an opportunity or resenting the disruption, inflated their prices. A three-person board was established to appraise properties and conduct negotiations. Ches Lyons's 1958 report noted that if all efforts failed, "expropriation action would be taken".[6]

It was a difficult process. Lives were being disrupted and most being affected were elderly. Richard Wright describes it succinctly:

The first reconstructive years were not without problems, disappointments, misunderstandings and lack of sensitivity. To Ludditt's chagrin, the restoration did not proceed as he and other old timers had planned. There was little communication between

In November 1973, I arrived back in Barkerville intending to stay a few months, the winter at most. My husband and I had a hand-built camper on the back of our truck. The campgrounds being closed, we parked for a few days in the main lot close to town. There was already three feet of snow and the temperature was well below zero. On a crisp moonlit night we walked through the streets of Barkerville. I knew nothing of the 15 years of work that had already gone into preserving this relic; I only knew that I could feel time slipping again. I also didn't know that I would soon join the team of passionate crusaders who were trying to bring this experience to others and that Barkerville would become part of my life for the next 40 years.

||||||||||||||||||||||||||||||||||||||||||||||

THE ORIGINAL CONCEPT for the recreated Barkerville was to present the town authentically as it looked between 1869 and 1885 – after the Great Fire of 1868. There was also to be a fire-proof museum to house newly acquired artifacts and an outdoor museum to display mining machinery. These, along with modern services such as campgrounds, would be around the periphery of the "old town".

The intent of the restoration was to commemorate that original mad rush of miners into the hinterland, the influx necessitating the formation of a Crown colony to protect British interests. But by 1869 the initial rush was over and many prospectors were moving on to more hopeful prospects. The restored town would actually represent the more stable and planned community that was built around the mining of the deeper deposits – ventures that required more time, more manpower and more capital. Nonetheless, much of the early iconography of the restored town was based on the idea of the prospector, and early marketing promoted the excitement of the initial gold rush.

Initially, the presentation of the town was somewhat static. During the inaugural 1958 season, for an initial cost of $1000, plywood signs with what Ches Lyons called a "rustic border treatment" and a style of printing that "helped enhance the pioneer atmosphere" were erected at strategic places throughout the town site. Static displays were created with wire screen gates, so the public could see in but not enter. Mannequins lent "a good deal of colour and interest to exhibit buildings". These mannequins were lifelike enough to startle more than a few visitors over the next 25 years.[8] Uniformed tour guides were introduced by the early 1970s, allowing the visitor to become more involved in learning the Barkerville story.

But the story of Barkerville was much more complex and multi-layered than just the initial gold rush. There were actually several gold rushes in BC. Whenever global finances dipped, interest in gold rose. The 1890s saw significant new activity in the Barkerville area, as did the Great Depression in the 1930s.

As the restoration work at Barkerville continued, research revealed layers and layers of information. Building investigations uncovered many surprises – older buildings within the walls of what was thought to be more recent buildings, an entire cabin buried by mine tailings beneath the surface of the current town. Carefully peeling wallpaper from the walls of the old buildings often uncovered even more interesting treasures underneath such as the 19th-century theatre posters found in the Kelly Saloon or the newspapers in St Saviour's Church. The lives of famous Barkerville personalities were found to be more complex as well. Researchers discovered that Billy Barker had left a

Lottie Bowron has tea with a mannequin in the parlour of her father's recreated house in Barkerville, about 1960.
Barkerville Archives P7596

wife and daughter back in England and in fact had living descendants. The story of the Kelly family was not confined to the story of Elizabeth Kelly walking up the snowy Cariboo trail with her hoop skirts hitched up to her ears but continued over several generations interwoven with the stories of the McKinnons, the Browns and the Tregilluses. But this treasure trove of stories remained within the walls of the Barkerville Archives. Out on the street the main story was the initial gold rush. The master plan completed in the early 1980s narrowed the historic period to be portrayed by the costumed interpreters to the year 1870.

The idea of historic costumes outside the theatrical presentations at Barkerville was slow to develop. When a site manager in the mid 1970s was approached about the guides, who were usually women, wearing historic costumes, he expressed his fear that young women wearing long dresses would be mistaken for hippies. These fears were alleviated when one of the older employees sported a green 1870s bustle dress constructed from an original pattern. Soon all the guides appeared on the streets in appropriate attire and this authenticity in costuming became a hallmark of Barkerville.

The link with the hippie movement of the 1970s was not as far-fetched as it sounds, though. In her book *All Roads Lead to Wells*, Susan Safyan writes:

> Barkerville, then firmly dedicated to faithfully recreating the 1870s, fostered employees who were keen to learn nearly forgotten pre-industrial skills such as wheelwrighting, log house restoration and building, carpentry using hand tools, or blacksmithing – skills that were making a comeback in the early 1970s.[9]

These skills were of great interest to a generation that was seeking a less materialistic lifestyle, and many youthful Barkerville employees considered themselves part of this movement.

Barkerville staff was also influenced by the 'living history' approach to museum interpretation which, while it could be traced back to the late 19th century in Scandinavia, was emerging in North America in the 1970s. This approach used

costumed 'interpreters' or 'animators' recreating everyday tasks to bring the artifacts and buildings of the past to life.

The practice of living history gained credence during the new social history movement of the 1960s and 1970s, and bicentennial fervour helped make costumed interpreters synonymous with vibrant programming at museums such as Plimoth Plantation and Old Sturbridge Village in Massachusetts and Colonial Williamsburg, Virginia.[10]

By 1980 all workers in the Barkerville heritage area were living in 1870. Personas were chosen, either real or fictional, and carefully researched. All interaction was in character. The *Cariboo Sentinel* newspaper from 1870 was read for timely news and local slang expressions. And role players recreated events that occurred that year in Barkerville.

It is 11 pm on an August evening in 1983, or is it 1870? The Wake Up Jake Coffee Saloon is bursting with revellers. Guitar, mandolin and harmonica music spills out into the street and reverberates off the buildings. The Williams Creek Fire Brigade Ball is in full swing. I have stepped out onto the boardwalk to catch my breath after a vigorous polka. My corset is far too tight and my button boots hurt my feet. Again that all too familiar prickling sensation at the back of my neck. Tonight it is not so much that time has slipped but that we have awakened the spirits. I have this vision of the inhabitants up in the cemetery raising their heads as if from sleep and asking: "Is that music I hear? Sounds like it's coming from the Jake. Come on, boys we'd better get down there."

Ron Candy in 1976 with the new Barkerville *Edukit* that he designed and built with colleagues Judy Campbell and Clarence Wood. Barkerville Archives BP0846

BARKERVILLE IS NOW A DESTINATION for school groups. The gold rush is part of the Grade 5 curriculum in BC. In the early years, buses would pull into the parking lot unannounced and disgorge groups of 40 or more children making a bee-line straight for the bakery and the "root beer saloon". Sometimes tours were organized for them, but generally the groups did not pre-book, and it was clear that Barkerville was being underused as an educational resource. There was so much at Barkerville to fuel the imagination of children. They loved panning for gold and riding the stagecoach because they were living the history rather than just being told about it. The question was: How could you bring those dusty old artifacts out from behind glass barriers and into their lives?

During the winter of 1975–76 the first Barkerville education kit was researched, designed and constructed. The intent was to take Barkerville to schools all over the province, many too far away for children to visit. A reconstructed steamer trunk with a hand-forged lock opened to reveal pictures, games, a slide show and even a miniature rocker box that could be used to find the gold contained in

a small bag of gravel. The kit was an overnight success and was soon booked three years in advance, so additional kits were constructed. Soon six kits were in circulation across the province, and their popularity continues to this day.

This hands-on approach was soon adopted for on-site education. An ambitious program was developed for the 1976 season: students would live in Barkerville for a day, spending half the day in the Wendle House cooking a lunch of beans and bannock, hauling wood and water, learning Victorian parlour games and manners, and doing early crafts such as quilting. After lunch they would go mining, which included the use of a rocker box and panning for gold, and go to work in the Holt & Burgess Cabinetry Shop working on a Cariboo tipper chair. The Wendle House program was an instant success and was completely booked in its first season.

Encouraged by this success, Barkerville staff went on to develop more participatory programs and the 1977 season saw students enjoying a period lesson with a strict Victorian teacher in the Williams Creek School House and acting out an original trial at the Richfield Courthouse.

By 1978 the programs had become so popular that when bookings opened for the upcoming season, the phone rang off the hook and within a few hours they were completely subscribed. School visitation went from a few hundred students in the early 1970s to 4195 in 1980, and it remains in the thousands today.

But there were challenges to adopting a strict living-history approach, trying to capture a moment in time – 1870. For one thing, there was precious little that actually dated from that time period. Although there were buildings from the period of 1869 to 1885, many buildings from later time periods lined the streets – the Wendle and

Will Bowron houses from the 1890s, the house of the famous Cariboo lawyer Hub King from the 1930s, the Goldfields Bakery from the 1930s. And although many household furnishings changed little from 1850 to the turn of the century, furniture styles did, and it was proving very difficult to furnish dozens of displays accurately.

Most of the animated displays were in buildings from later time periods, which were made to look as close to 1870 as possible. This posed dilemmas for the animators when they were asked about the building and its previous owners. Interpreters soon found ways to foreshadow the future and talk to visitors about Barkerville's full story while staying in their 19th-century persona.

The research necessary to recreate a strict 1870s streetscape uncovered some fascinating building histories. The Nicol Hotel, for instance, was originally a one-storey building built by the Kwong Lee Company on a lot across the street from its current location on the main street of Barkerville. Fanny Bendixen occupied it from 1880 until her death in 1899. A second storey was added, and then in 1915 the building was moved to Chinatown. A few years later it was moved to its current location. Buildings such as the Kibbee and Nason houses had additions and lean-tos, and each portion of the house dated from a different time period.

As fascinating as this research was, the intent was to return buildings to what they were in the 1870s. In the process, non-conforming additions were removed to reveal the portions of the building that fit within the proscribed time period. Although these removals were carefully documented with samples and photographs, it was felt by some that an important part of Barkerville history was being lost. The gold rush of the 1890s was characterized by advances in mining technology. Was this not also important to British Columbians? Were not the stories of the Wendles, Kibbees and Leiscester Bonner significant?

Philosophies in the museum community were changing. Focus on social history was leading to a much more layered approach to heritage preservation. When Bill Quackenbush became curator at Barkerville in 1990, he not only realized that Barkerville did not have enough artifacts to accurately portray 1870, but knew that there were many important and interesting stories that needed to be told about the later periods in the town's history.

The next few years saw a transition from interpreting Barkerville as a "moment in time" to telling the full story of community-building that spanned 100 years. Each building had its own story to tell, sometimes multiple stories. Displays within buildings would represent an important period during the building's life, but not necessarily the 1800s. Some buildings would tell the stories from the 1930s and '40s.

The challenge for the costumed interpreters was considerable. Would not the visitors become confused meeting characters from the 1860s and the 1930s on the street at the same time? Surprisingly, this ripple in the space/time continuum does not disturb the visitors; after all, they have already tacitly agreed to 'believe' in time travel. The visitors enjoy their personal contact with all the characters and their stories.

Barkerville's fame as a tourist attraction brought more than 100,000 visitors annually through the 1970s. This was the era of the family road trip vacation, and Barkerville had all the ingredients – history, adventure, camping and the outdoors, and of course gold! In today's world of cheap airfare and family vacations to all-inclusives in warmer climes, Barkerville along with heritage

Nozzle used in hydraulic mining near Barkerville in the late 1800s. RBCM 972.4.73

attractions world-wide, has seen diminishing visitation.

But Barkerville holds many other treasures and offers many more opportunities. Its collection of more than 200,000 artifacts, photos and archival records is of international significance. The need for a museum to house the most precious artifacts and to provide an orientation to the site was recognized in the earliest plans. The original resolution presented by Bill Speare to the Legislative Assembly resolved, "That immediate official effort on the part of Government be undertaken to safe-guard loss of museum objects by negotiation or purchase where required."[11] The report made to the Centennial Committee in the fall of 1958, after the first season of operation, made a further recommendation: "The high value of historical exhibits makes it almost mandatory that a permanent fire-proof building be built for a museum and storage area."[12]

The Kelly Museum, which had been started by George Kelly, grandson of pioneers Andrew and Elizabeth Kelly, was purchased in 1958. It included a significant collection of gold-rush memorabilia that was on the verge of being sold to an American museum, including a broad axe stamped with "Barker Co" and presumed to belong to Billy Barker. A publicity campaign was launched to encourage people to donate. Ches Lyons put out the call in an article written by Art Downs in the *Northwest Digest*:

This project belongs to all of BC and it is something in which everyone may participate. There is hardly a home that hasn't got something of value for us. An entire town has to be rebuilt and furnished, and thousands of articles are going to be required.... We have already received dozens of items from people interested in the restoration program. For instance, we recently received from Mrs Arthur Haddock of Williams Lake, Billy Barker's watch and two of his gold pokes.[13]

This campaign brought in thousands of artifacts, which were used for museum displays and to populate the dozens of period rooms on the site – and to fill up every nook and cranny of storage space that could be found.

With the advent of computer technology and years of cataloguing efforts, this collection has become more accessible to researchers. Under the auspices of the new Barkerville Conservation and Learning Institute, new storage areas have been completed. Partnerships have been developed with the major universities. For instance, the significance of Barkerville's Chinese collections has been recognized on both sides of the Pacific. Barkerville has one of the largest collections of Chinese documents specific to pre-railway activities in North America. In 2012 Barkerville mounted a groundbreaking exhibit of photographs and stories of the Chinese pioneers who travelled back to their home towns in southern China. The exhibit features a database of over 1300 photographs with an interactive kiosk that allows visitors to add information in either English or Chinese. Research partnerships have been established with the Guangdong Museum of Overseas Chinese in Guanzhou and Wuyi University in Jiangmen. As well, the University of Northern BC and Barkerville co-hosted a significant academic symposium in 2012, and the resulting papers will be published in a special Barkerville edition of *BC Studies* in 2015.

Barkerville remains a special place for every visitor. I love to watch wide-eyed children as they find that first fleck of gold in their pan. I love to watch older people as they recognize household items from their youth. My favourite is men, often from the prairies, discussing a large piece of industrial equipment, figuring out how it probably worked. If I ever have doubts about the value of heritage, the worth of preserving sites like Barkerville for future generations, I just need to spend some time watching the visitors, overhearing their conversations as they process their experience, watching the children's faces. It is all worth it. ⚒

ACKNOWLEDGEMENTS

Barkerville Historic Town has attracted a long and impressive list of extremely talented and creative people who have made contributions to its development over the years. To name any would be to exclude others equally worthy, so I will name none. But more than anything else, the contributions of the staff and volunteers have shaped Barkerville and made it the success it is today. Special thanks to the staff in the Barkerville Archives for their assistance in preparing this article.

NOTES

1   Original spelling.

2   Fred Ludditt. *Barkerville Days* (Langley: Mr Paperback), 1980 (revised edition), p. 150.

3   C.P. Lyons, *Report on Barkerville Project made for the BC Centennial Committee*, 1958, p. 2. Barkerville Archives.

4   Taralee Alcock, "From Living to History: The Transition of Barkerville, BC, to the Barkerville Historic Town in the Bennett Era". Unpublished paper submitted for *UNBC History 407*, 1996, p. 11. Barkerville Archives.

5   C.P. Lyons, correspondence to W. Kelly, September 8, 1959, Barkerville Archives, vertical file "Park History".

6   Lyons, Report on Barkerville Project, p. 3.

7   R.T. Wright. *Barkerville and the Cariboo Goldfields* (Vancouver: Heritage House), 2013, p. 129, containing quotation from Ludditt, *Barkerville Days*, p. 155.

8   Lyons, *Report on Barkerville Project*, p. 3.

9   Susan Safyan, *All Roads Lead to Wells* (Halfmoon Bay, BC: Caitlin Press), 2012, p. 187.

10 The Association of Living History, Farm and Agricultural Museums (ALHFAM) website, www.almfam.org.

11 Resolution presented to Legislative Assembly by Bill Speare. Barkerville Archives.

12 Lyons, *Report on Barkerville Project*, p. 2.

13 Art Downs, "Look What's Happening to Barkerville", *Northwest Digest*, December 1959.

The Gold Rush and Confederation

Lorne Foster Hammond

||||||||||||||||||||||||||||||||||||||||||||||||||

THE STORY of how British Columbia entered Confederation and became a province is, on the surface, well known but emphasizes the view from the seat of the colonial government. It goes something like this: Worried about American expansion and encumbered by a falling population and debts from gold-rush road construction, after much debate and influenced by a new governor sent from London to promote Confederation, the Colony of British Columbia dispatched a three-person delegation to Ottawa in 1870.

The delegation was led by British Columbia's Chief Commissioner of Lands Joseph Trutch. With him went Dr John S. Helmcken, previously an opponent of Confederation, who would handle questions of finance. As Helmcken left the only account, his view dominates. He was concerned that if the colony joined Canada they would lose their largest single source of revenue – the taxes and duties on imported goods. The third delegation member was from Barkerville. Dr Robert W.W. Carrall represented the Cariboo, and he receives minimal comment in most histories.

The trio of negotiators sailed from Victoria to San Francisco on May 14 on board the steamer *Active*, which had carried gold and miners on the Fraser River in 1858. Five days later they landed in San Francisco to take the first of a series of American railways that would carry them through the mountains and across the plains to Chicago and then north to Canada. It was the first year of the USA's newly finished transcontinental rail system. A railway line across Canada became a clearly practical idea on that railway trip.

Arriving in Ottawa on June 3 the delegation was well received. Prime Minister John A. Macdonald was not available, so the negotiations were conducted by George Etienne Cartier, who hosted the delegation. Initial negotiations with the Privy Council were intense and detailed and ran until June 8, dealing with the larger complex issues of debt, railways and subsidies. Then the negotiations broke off for the arrival of the Prince of Wales in Quebec City and his Canadian tour. Negotiations resumed on June 25 to finish the more minor clauses.

An engineer by trade, Trutch got down to business with the Privy Council negotiating investments of infrastructure for harbours and questions relating to land. Today he is remembered for how he misrepresented the existing liberal treatment of First Nations, but Helmcken mentions in his diary:

The clause about Indians was very fully discussed. The Ministers thought our system better than theirs in some respects but what system would be adopted remained for the future to determine. I asked about Indian Wars and Sir G. Cartier said it depended on the severity, as a rule the expense would have to be borne by the Dominion Govt.[1]

For his part, Helmcken struck an agreement to help the underpopulated colony retire its gold rush road debts, and resolve the fiscal problem of lost import duties. The delegation, originally asking for a wagon road and telegraph, was surprised when their hosts suggested a railway might be possible. Cartier suggested that a belt of land along the railway be transferred by the province to offset the cost of the railway.

After much discussion and general introductions to the members of Parliament, the delegation

returned to Victoria with a viable proposal to present to the Legislature, which after more debate, was adopted. News came from Ottawa that the motion there had been approved.

On July 20, 1871, British Columbia became the sixth province in Canada. The colonial governor departed and Trutch accepted the constitutional post at the head of the province's legal structure as the first Lieutenant-Governor. But even in office he continued to hope that he could be the project engineer to build the new railway to Canada across the Rockies, and he had the support of Prime Minister John A. Macdonald.[2] Those plans would fall apart when the Pacific Railway scandal brought down the Conservative government, and it would not be until the 1880s that the railway promise would be kept.

Far left: Joseph William Trutch, British Columbia's first Lieutenant-Governor, 1871. Lambert Weston and Son photograph; BCA A-01004

Centre: In 1863 Joseph Trutch built the first Alexandra Bridge just above Yale on the Fraser River on the road to the Cariboo. For many years he received payment in tolls (the tollhouse is on the left). BCA E-03960

Above: Dr John Helmcken in Ottawa, 1870. William J. Topley photograph; BCA A-01351

Previous spread: Judge Joseph Needham and party at Carrall's Grouse Creek cabin in September 1867. Frederick Dally photograph; BCA A-01842

Of the three delegates who negotiated our entry into Confederation, history has been kind to Helmcken and not so kind to Trutch. But it is to remedy the neglect to the third delegate that this essay now turns. Robert Carrall is undeservedly an almost forgotten man. What was his background? What role did he play in British Columbia joining Canada? It turns out the answer is very closely connected to the gold rush, and the mining town of Barkerville.

Dr Robert William Weir Carrall (1839–79) was the fifth son of a United Empire Loyalist family at Carrall's Grove, near Woodstock, Ontario. (One branch of the Carrall family had signed the US Declaration of Independence, but his grandfather chose to take his family north.) When Robert Carrall was born his family lived in Upper Canada; but when he was just two years of age, the region became known as Canada West.

Because he was born in Canada, Carrall felt comfortable with the idea of Confederation, because it meant rejoining, not abandoning his identity. (He was the only Canadian in the delegation to Ottawa – both Trutch and Helmcken were born in England.) Joining Confederation was a view Carrall shared with many gold-rush immigrants, including many who came overland or by sea. Key newspaper editors such as John Robson and Amor de Cosmos were born in the other provinces and all were critical of the old fur-trade society and the British imperial adherents. In the Confederation debates in colonial British Columbia, the biggest resistance was not from pro-Americans but from those unwilling to let go of British imperial attachments. Even Governor Frederick Seymour was uneasy about the idea.[3]

Carrall was not afraid of the future: he cherished those eastern connections. Nor was he afraid of new technological or economic change. He saw his first train not on that historic trip to Ottawa in 1870, but almost two decades earlier. He was 13 when his family greeted the arrival of the Great Western Railway, which connected Woodstock with the rest of Upper Canada in 1852. It had carried him to college, then medical school, and to war. On their way to Ottawa, Carrall and Helmcken stopped in Woodstock and at a welcoming banquet, Helmcken, newly converted by Carrall and the railway experience, spoke with great enthusiasm of the West and the untold wealth of British Columbia, arguing that to develop "a railroad is a necessity".[4]

CARRALL'S EARLY LIFE

ROBERT CARRALL began his medical studies at Trinity College in Toronto in 1853 and in July 1857 transferred to medicine at Montreal's famed McGill medical college. Like Guy's Hospital in

London where Dr Helmcken trained, McGill was a hotbed of new teaching ideas. Students learned while working on the wards with living patients. It was at McGill that Carrall met Israel Wood Powell, a fellow medical student from Ontario. He was a Mason and, like Carrall, supported John A. Macdonald's Conservatives. Powell would become Carrall's close friend and mentor; downtown Vancouver now has a street named for each man.

Carrall graduated fourth in a class of twenty-one in May 1859, and returned home to open a surgery in Woodstock. Following the example of Powell and his own father, he joined the local Masonic Lodge. Then tragedy struck. Like Dr Helmcken, who was unable to save his wife Cecilia, Carrall could not save his mother, Jane Weir Carrall, who died in December 1861. The next year, seeking change, Robert Carrall left Woodstock, taking a contract for $100 a month as a medical officer in the American Union Army.

He travelled south on the train to Buffalo and then to Washington, DC, where he signed his medical service contract.

From 1862 to 1865 Carrall served as an assistant surgeon. He spent the first year at Emory, one of many large Washington hospitals treating casualties of the US Civil War. He may or may not have gone on to serve in a field hospital, but he re-emerges in the historical record in 1864 on staff at a large military hospital in New Orleans. Exhausted by what he had seen of the bloody civil war and shocked at the assassination of Lincoln, Carrall gave notice to end his contract. Like many veterans weary of war, he took the train west looking for peaceful opportunities but with no clear goal in mind.

Arriving in San Francisco, Carrall visited the local Freemason lodge and heard stories of the opportunities in Alaska, newly purchased from

Russia, and news of the Fraser River and Cariboo gold rush. He saw British-flagged ships in the harbour and learned of a contract on Vancouver Island for a doctor to treat coal miners.

He took passage north to Victoria on the SS *Commodore* and settled briefly in Nanaimo, taking the medical contract with the Vancouver Coal Mining and Land Company. While there he joined the Nanaimo Volunteer Rifle Corps, as well as amateur musical and theatre groups. He also joined Nanaimo's new Scottish Freemason Lodge, No. 1090. These fraternal organizations were central to community building and politics in gold rush societies. It is no coincidence that many of the Canadian-born proponents for Confederation were also Masonic Lodge members.

On a brief visit to Victoria in the spring of 1866, Carrall was surprised to find his old friend Dr Israel Powell. Powell had been on his way to New Zealand via Panama when he arrived in 1862 to find a prosperous gold-rush town in need of a doctor. Now elected to the legislature, Powell led a pro-Canada party. He introduced Carrall to John Helmcken and the Victoria merchants who invested in the gold fields. Powell, Helmcken and their merchant friends liked Carrall and his politics. They suggested that there were opportunities for him up in the Cariboo.

Powell had a key influence on Carrall. The colonial era of Governor James Douglas was ending, yet the new colonial government was dominated by a paternalistic British colonial mindset. Powell argued for Canadian-style electoral reform, promoting the idea of union with his Canada Party. Powell's father and grandfather had both been members of the legislature in

Canada West and Conservative Prime Minister John A. Macdonald, a family friend, had given Powell a letter of introduction.[5] He convinced Carrall to write directly to Macdonald about the need for BC to join Confederation, and to lead the cause in Barkerville, the centre of the gold economy.

CARRALL IN BARKERVILLE

IN 1864, prospectors found a major source of gold in narrow Grouse Creek, about five kilometres south of Barkerville. Victorian merchant stock-holders funded the Grouse Creek Bedrock Flume Company to build a large flume to divert the water from the claim to get access to its hundreds of

ounces of gold waiting to be shovelled out. But in the fall of 1866 the company ran out of capital and work was abandoned. During one of his regular visits to Victoria, Robert Carrall purchased a cabin on Grouse Creek, sight unseen, from one of the company shareholders. He decided to go there and establish himself.

In December 1866, as his contract ended with the Vancouver Coal Mining and Land Company, Carrall made plans to go up to the Cariboo. Before he left he attended a mass meeting over the location for the new United Colony's capital: should it be in Victoria or New Westminster? The crowded theatre heard from John Helmcken, Robert Burnaby, Amor de Cosmos, Selim Franklin and many others. Carrall seconded the resolution that the people should vote on the location of the capital of the newly

United Colony of British Columbia. It should not be an arbitrary decision of a colonial governor.[6] Later that month he showed his support at the annual dinner of the French Benevolent Society.[7] He was well connected politically even before he reached the gold fields and the Hotel France.

Carrall probably arrived in Barkerville before March, when the mining season began. He would find his new cabin in the middle of a conflict over mining rights. The Grouse Creek Bedrock Flume Company had ceased operations in the previous fall because it could not afford to pay for the materials and dozens of labourers required to build flumes and tunnels. Another group of miners, called the Canadian Company, was granted the claim and began to work it.

In the spring when Carrall arrived, the Grouse Creek Flume Company applied to get its claim back, but the Canadian Company refused to vacate a claim they had been legally given. The issue quickly escalated into a standoff. Forty miners, angry at local mining courts and Judge Begbie's refusal to hear their appeal, refused to leave.[8]

On July 16, 1867, Magistrate Henry Maynard Ball and 25 constables served a notice to vacate, but the miners refused to leave. This tense scene was being watched by a crowd of 400 other miners, so the constables declined to arrest the protesters. A telegram was sent to the governor to request that the Royal Navy send marines, but the navy refused to become involved.

Accusations, not bullets, flew between the groups in the Cariboo and in Victoria newspapers. In August Governor Frederick Seymour arrived in Barkerville to investigate what the papers had begun to call "the Grouse Creek War".[9] A group of Canadian Company miners agreed to go briefly to jail, but the door was not to be locked and drink was provided. The governor appointed Supreme Court Judge Joseph Needham to arbitrate the dispute. After two weeks of hearings, he found for the Grouse Creek Bedrock Flume Company, ending the so-called war.

Dr Carrall set up his medical practice, accepted shares for services and invested his money. Unlike many other investors, he was fortunate. He became a partner in not one but two very profitable claims on Williams Creek, the most famous being the lucrative Minnehaha Claim.

By 1868 Dr Carrall had become a popular figure in Barkerville. Outgoing and lively, he established himself at the social core of the small but busy gold rush town. His musical skills, love of dancing and social events, and enthusiasm for amateur theatre fit in well. His Freemason views on community-building, business, harmony and free education also met with approval. His name appears frequently in the *Cariboo Sentinel*, the Barkerville newspaper, as

a supporter of community activities. Carrall spent a lot of time talking about politics and the question of union with Canada. On November 23, 1867, he chaired a large town-hall meeting in Barkerville that passed a resolution in favour of Confederation. He declared: "We will span a continent with a cordon of thinking, energetic, pulsating humanity, and a railroad will follow."[10]

In September 16, 1868, at 2 p.m. a fire broke out at Addler and Barrie's billiard hall. The cause was likely a stove pipe; but popular Barkerville folklore about a miner's pursuit of a kiss is not mentioned in the newspaper account published immediately after the event.[11] Carrall's home was on the west side of the street, next to the Barnard Express office and two doors down from the Masonic Lodge went up in flames. The loss of his home was valued at $500. Within a few hours 116 buildings, including

30 in Barkerville's Chinatown, burned to the ground. Only 20 per cent of the town remained, but rebuilding began almost immediately.

A month after the fire Robert Carrall was elected without opposition as the Cariboo's representative in the colonial Legislature in Victoria.[12] His platform was clear: to speak for the Cariboo, to promote Confederation, to lobby for a railway connection to Canada, and to emphasize the need for Canada to spread from sea to sea to compete with the United States for immigration. He served as the representative for the Cariboo until 1871.

From his small office Carrall wrote a steady stream of letters to Sir John A. Macdonald to tell him of the support in the gold fields for union with Canada. He advised him on the mood in the region and suggested ways of moving confederation forward. John A Macdonald wrote back congratulating him on his election, providing advance advice on plans for confederation and told him to keep "the Union fire alight until it burns over the entire Colony".[13]

One mechanism Carrall used with great effect to promote union with Canada was to organize a celebration of Dominion Day in Barkerville. The program for the event held at Barkerville on July 1, 1869, included horse races with a silver Queen's Plate and a Dominion Day cup, and a velocipede race.[14]

Sir John A. Macdonald.
BCA C-09046

Apparently his lack of skill on the new velocipede (an early bicycle) provided laughter for his friends.

Earlier that year a new colonial governor had been sent from Britain to encourage Confederation with Canada, which also had the quiet support of John A. Macdonald. Governor Anthony Musgrave brought Carrall into the executive council in the winter of 1870. In April 1862 Musgrave selected him as the third member of the delegation to represent the British Columbia Legislature to negotiate terms for joining Canada.

Carrall promoted the advantages of British Columbia's coal, lumber, gold, silver and copper resources. Mining meant wealth and a bright western future for Canada. He spoke directly from experience living in the gold fields, and also for the wider idea of the resource economy and its future. His background with Barkerville mining syndicates made him the perfect counsellor to talk to businessmen and investors about opportunities in British Columbia.

His 20 years of ease with railroad travel and his Woodstock and Montreal roots also made him the perfect promoter for the idea of a practical connection from sea to sea. His American experience allowed him to talk knowingly about rail competition, risks of annexation or Fenian invasions (a topic of the moment in Ottawa, as was Red River) and the question of Canada and the United States in the post-Civil War world.

Carrall spoke eloquently and enthusiastically for Confederation. And he had all the right political connections to win over support. He was a Canadian. He had connections in Ontario and Montreal, the support of Powell's political friends and the Freemasons, and the backing of Governor Musgrave. But most tellingly, he was the only member of the delegation that was granted a private interview with Sir John A. Macdonald.

The delegation's three weeks of meetings were successful. Carrall stayed to visit family, and Helmcken returned to brief the colonial legislature. As Helmcken records it, it was all rather matter of fact, with very little celebration. News followed from Ottawa by telegraph that Canada had endorsed the terms of union, and so had BC's last colonial legislature. On July 20, 1871, British Columbia became the sixth province to join Canada. The last colonial governor departed five days later, before the new Lieutenant-Governor was appointed.

In December two members of the BC negotiation team for Confederation were offered Senate appointments. Carrall accepted his appointment, but Helmcken declined and returned to medicine.[15] The third delegate, Joseph Trutch, was appointed Lieutenant-Governor. Carrall's return trip to Ottawa followed the same San Francisco route as he'd taken with Helmcken and Trutch the year before. On his way to Ottawa he again stopped to see family at Woodstock and received a public reception.[16] The member from Barkerville and the Cariboo took his seat on April 11, 1872, as one of three new senators from British Columbia.[17]

Unfortunately, Carrall never lived to see the completion of the railway he promoted. He'd been a social butterfly and confirmed bachelor for most of his life, but when his health declined sharply he realized how serious his medical condition was, so he quietly married his childhood Woodstock sweetheart, Elizabeth Amelia Macdonald Gordon. They were married in Ottawa on May 8, 1879, and Robert Carrall died at Carrall's Grove near Woodstock four months later on September 19 at the age of 40.

His last achievement, the passage of his private member's Dominion Day Bill, was close to his heart.[18] He saw it as a vehicle of unity and harmony, across regional interests. The lone voice to speak out against the bill was a fellow Conservative senator from BC, Francis Cornwall, who pointed out that the promise of a railway had still not been delivered. But Carrall's bill passed and July 1 became the official holiday to celebrate Canada, an event Carrall organized and celebrated in Barkerville in 1869. In the debate for the bill just before his last summer he said:

I have always loved the Dominion dearly. I helped to found it. I have worked since with all the energy I possessed by vote and voice to consolidate it. I think we should have one day which should be observed throughout the Dominion as the anniversary of Confederation. Like the mighty empire of Rome, some part is always in rebellion. British Columbia is restive and irritated. Now is the time to legislate the Dominion into one harmonious whole…. I speak my own feelings, claiming to be a patriotic Canadian.[19]

History lives in the retelling. The events of these people of the Gold Rush shaped our identities, and our province and nation. They came for gold but made a country. ⚒

ACKNOWLEDGEMENTS

Written with a deep scholarly debt and appreciation of the contributions of these outstanding historians: Dr Willard Ireland, Dr Dorothy Blakely Smith, Dr W.G. Sheldon and the Hon. Brian Smith, and Dr Tina Loo. A special thanks to Isabella Crawford-Siano of Woodstock, Ontario, historian and author of *Senator Robert Carrall and Dominion Day* (Woodstock: Quarry Heritage Books), 2011, the only full biography of Carrall. My thanks also to the staff of the British Columbia Archives and the National Archives of Canada.

NOTES

1   J.S. Helmcken, Confederation Diary, in *The Reminiscences of Doctor John Sebastian Helmcken*, edited by Dorothy Blakey Smith (Vancouver: UBC Press), 1975, p. 357. Trutch personally saw First Nations as an impediment to European settlement. He disagreed with Governor James Douglas's policy, and after Douglas retired, Trutch had worked to shrink the size of reserves.

2   "I have gathered from you that your ambition is to be charged with the very interesting work of constructing the Railway through British Columbia and the Rocky Mountains. I have no doubt of being able, from my influence with the Board to secure you this appointment and I have no doubt the remuneration will be fixed at a satisfactory rate." PAC John A. Macdonald fonds. Letter Book 19, 770, Macdonald to Joseph Trutch, February 13, 1873. From Margaret Ormsby, "Canada and the New British Columbia, fn. 33, p. 105 in *Readings in British Columbia History*, edited by J. Freisen and H.K. Ralston (Kingston-Montreal: McGill-Queen's University Press), 1976.

3   The early BC Historian F.W. Howay would put it even more strongly, that Seymour was against the idea. See: F.W. Howay, "The Attitude of Governor Seymour towards Confederation," In *Transactions of the Royal Society of Canada*, 3rd series, XIV, Sec ii, 1921, pp. 31-51.

4 An account of a dinner speech making a railway the key to the negotiations appeared later in the *Globe*, June 10, 1870, cited in Brian Smith, "The Confederation Delegation," *British Columbia and Confederation*, edited by W. George Shelton (Victoria: Morriss Printing for the University of Victoria), 1967, p. 202.

5 See B.A. McKelvie, "Lieutenant-Colonel Israel Wood Powell, M.D. *British Columbia Historical Quarterly*, XI January 1947, p. 34.

6 "Mass Meeting," *British Colonist*, January 8, 1867, p. 2.

7 "The Anniversary Dinner of the French Benevolent Society, British Colonist, January 20, 1867, p. 3.

8 The eviction hearing was held on April 22, 1867 and the Canadians initially complied but returned at the end of May to continue their work. Warren Spalding, the Assistant Gold Commissioner had granted the claim to both groups at different times. June saw events come to a head as the Victoria-based Grouse Creek Flume Company laid trespass charges. See "Trespassing on Grouse Creek Bed Rock Flume Co.'s Ground" and also "Magistrate's Court," *Cariboo Sentinel*, 3 June 1867. The problems of Mining Law and the events leading up to details of the trial *Canadian Company v. Grouse Creek Flume Co., Ltd*, September 27, 1867, are explored in depth by Dr Tina Loo in her article "*A Delicate Game: The Meaning of Law on Grouse Creek*", BC Studies 96 (Winter 1992–93, pp. 41-65.)

9 The use of the term is found here: "*The Grouse Creek War*," *British Colonist*, 29 July 1867. Was it deserved? The supporters of the Canada Company pointed out that it was Victoria, where the owners of the Grouse Creek Flume Company were based, that fanned the flames with rhetoric, not the peaceful streets of Barkerville. Locally the events were simply seen as miners standing up for their legal rights to a claim, now removed without appeal, seen as an injustice in mining law. That view is expressed in articles like "The Governor and the Grouse Creek Difficulty," *Cariboo Sentinel*, 12 August 1867.

10 Cited by Dorothy Blakey Smith, "Robert William Weir Carrall," *Dictionary of Canadian Biography*, vol. 10, (1871–80), University of Toronto Press, http://www.biographi.ca.

11 "Burning of Barkerville," *Cariboo Sentinel*, September 22, 1868.

12 "Returned," *British Colonist*, October 27, 1868, p. 3.

13 Public Archive of Canada. Macdonald Papers, Letterbook 12, 367, Macdonald to Carrall, January 5, 1869.

14 "Dominion Day," *Cariboo Sentinel*, 16 June 1869.

15 "The Senators", *British Colonist*, October 11, 1871, p. 3. Helmcken left politics so that he could spend more time with his children. See Helmcken to Macdonald, August 23, 1871, PAC MG26A. Extract in *The Reminiscences of Doctor John Sebastian Helmcken*, edited by Dorothy Blakey Smith (Vancouver: UBC Press), 1975, pp. xxv-xxvi.

16 "Personal", *British Colonist*, February 7, 1872, p. 3. "Our Representatives", *British Colonist*, February 25, 1872, p. 3, reported Carrall as still at Woodstock on the 23rd, while his travel companion, MP Henry Nathan Jr, Victoria, Canada's first Jewish member of the House of Commons, had gone on to Montreal. Both met again in Ottawa.

17 The other two new senators elected to represent specific regions of British Columbia were William John Macdonald (Victoria) and Francis Clement Cornwall (Ashcroft). All three were members of the Conservative Party.

18 The *British Colonist* reported it passed the Commons on May 16, 1879, p 3.

19 Dr Robert W.W. Carrall, Dominion Day Bill, Second Reading, April 2, 1879. Canada. Parliament. Senate. *Debates of the Canadian Senate*, Ottawa: Queen's Printer, 1879, p. 201.

Slim Jim or *The Parson Takes the Pot*
Rowland Lee, 1892.

Note the bag of gold coins on the gambler's lap and gold coins used in this poker game. Saloons, high stakes card games and professional gamblers followed in the wave of the gold rush.

The artist named his painting *Slim Jim*, but no one knows why he chose that name or who in the picture he's referring to. Lee's daughter provided the alternative title, which at least tells us who has the winning hand.
BCA PDP00292

The Authors

DON BOURDON has been involved in the museum and archives fields for 40 years in Alberta and BC. In 2013, he brought his expertise to bear as Curator of Images and Paintings at the Royal British Columbia Museum where he is dedicated to caring for and raising the profile of more than five million photographs, paintings, drawings and prints. His most recent publishing project for *BC Studies* examines Thomas Robson Pattullo, (1837-1879) Barkerville's gregarious miner-cum-mine owner, bon vivant and confederationist.

DR KATHRYN BRIDGE is a historian, archivist and curator at the Royal BC Museum. She has written several books on historical figures in BC, including *By Snowshoe, Buckboard & Steamer* (about BC's frontier women), which won the 1998 Lieutenant-Governor's Medal for Historical Writing, and most recently *Emily Carr in England* (2014).

JUDY CAMPBELL got her first "real" job in Barkerville in 1974. Over the next 14 years she worked in various capacities as interpreter, researcher, program coordinator and visitor services manager. She holds a master's degree in Planning from University of Calgary's Faculty of Environmental Design, and for 18 years was the principle of Ecogistics Consulting providing a variety of services to the heritage, recreation and tourism sectors. In 2006, she returned to Barkerville as chief executive officer until 2014.

LILY CHOW has written several books about Canadian Chinese history in British Columbia: *Sojourners in the North* (1996), *Chasing Their Dreams* (2000), *Legends of Four Chinese Sages* (2007) and *Blood and Sweat over the Railway Tracks* (2014). Her awards include the Jeanne Clarke Memorial Local History (1997) and two Queen Elizabeth II Jubilee Medals (2002 and 2012). She is a retired teacher with a master's degree in education.

DR TZU-I CHUNG is curator of history at the Royal British Columbia Museum. Her most recent publications can be found in academic journals *Museum and Society* and *BC Studies*, and other public venues. Her current research focuses on the intercultural food history of British Columbia within the context of historical, cultural and economic exchange between North America and Asia, and on transnational migration theories.

MARIE ELLIOTT has written two books about British Columbia's interior: *Gold and Grand Dreams, Cariboo East in the Early Years* (2000) and *Fort St James and New Caledonia, Where British Columbia Began* (2009), and recently completed a history of the Fraser and Cariboo gold rushes. She has a masters degree in History and is a board member of the Friends of the British Columbia Archives.

HÉCTOR GARCÍA BOTERO is an anthropologist at the Museo del Oro, Banco de la República, in Bogotá, Colombia, and co-curator of the renovation of the Museo Etnográfico in the Colombian Amazon. He has a master's degree in anthropology at the Universidad de los Andes in Bogotá. His recent studies are about heritage legislation and pre-Hispanic reparations.

DR LORNE HAMMOND is a history curator at the Royal British Columbia Museum. He has written extensively and curated museum exhibitions on variety of subjects related to BC history, including Italian communities, military units, constitutional history, food, surveying, toys and 1960s pop culture. His most recent book, cowritten with Robert Griffin, is *Stewards of the People's Forests: A Short History of the British Columbia Forest Service* (2014).

JENNIFER IREDALE is the recently retired director of the British Columbia Heritage Branch and former (for 24 years) curator of provincial historic sites in BC. She has written numerous articles on BC history and was an editor and author of *Enduring Threads: Ecclesiastical Textiles of St John the Divine Church, Yale, British Columbia, Canada*. Her work has been recognized by the BC Museums Association Golden Anniversary Service Award (2011) and in 2012 her appointment as a Fellow of the Cascadia Green Building Council.

DR DANIEL MARSHALL is a fifth generation British Columbian whose Cornish ancestors arrived during the Fraser River gold rush. He is an adjunct assistant professor of history at the University of Victoria and works with First Nations and the provincial and federal governments on land and resource issues. He has written extensively on First nations subjects and was host and historical consultant for the documentary *Canyon War: The Untold Story*.

JUAN PABLO QUINTERO GUZMÁN is an archaeologist at the Museo del Oro, Banco de la República, in Bogotá, Colombia. He has a master's degree in anthropology with emphasis in archaeology from Universidad de los Andes, Bogotá, and a postgraduate diploma in Mediterranean nautical archaeology from Universitat de Barcelona, Spain.

MARÍA ALICIA URIBE VILLEGAS has been director of the Museo del Oro, Banco de la República, in Bogotá, Colombia, since 2010, after working for 16 years there as archaeologist and curator. She has a master's degree in Artifact Studies from Institute of Archaeology, University College, London.

New Perspectives on the Gold Rush

Design and layout by Lara Minja, Lime Design. Typeset in Minion Pro 10.5/13.5 and 9.5/13.5.

Editing by Amy Reiswig and Gerry Truscott, with assistance from Don Bourdon and Alex Van Tol.

Production coordination by Gerry Truscott, with assistance from Don Bourdon and Erika Stenson.

Colour photographs by Shane Lighter, unless stated otherwise in captions. Digital photographic production by Shane Lighter and Kelly-Ann Turkington.

Index by Carol Hamill.

Library and Archives Canada Cataloguing in Publication

New perspectives on the gold rush / edited by Kathryn Bridge.

Includes bibliographical references and index.
ISBN 978-0-7726-6854-7 (paperback)

1. British Columbia – Gold discoveries. 2. British Columbia – History – 1849–1871. I. Bridge, Kathryn Anne, 1955–, editor II. Royal BC Museum, issuing body

FC3822.4.N49 2015   971.1'02   C2015-902402-1

Index